# PRESS BRAKE
# TECHNOLOGY

# PRESS BRAKE
# TECHNOLOGY

a guide to precision sheet metal bending

Steve D. Benson

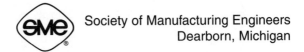

Society of Manufacturing Engineers
Dearborn, Michigan

Library of Congress Catalog Card Number: 96-070755
International Standard Book Number: 0-87263-483-3

Additional copies may be obtained by contacting:

Society of Manufacturing Engineers
Customer Service
One SME Drive
Dearborn, MI 48121
1-800-733-4763

SME staff who participated in producing this book:

Larry Binstock, Senior Editor
Rosemary Csizmadia, Operations Administrator
Frances Kania, Production Assistant
Judy Munro, Manager, Graphic Services
Dorothy Wylo, Production Assistant

Cover photo courtesy of The LVD Corporation


Printed in the United States of America

# ABOUT
# THE SOCIETY
# OF MANUFACTURING
# ENGINEERS

Founded in 1932, the Society of Manufacturing Engineers (SME) is a nonprofit professional society dedicated to the advancement of scientific knowledge in the field of manufacturing engineering. By providing direction for the evolution of manufacturing, SME has earned an international reputation for leadership in manufacturing technology.

Among its activities, SME produces and distributes a vast array of literature focusing on state-of-the-art, as well as traditional manufacturing techniques. *Press Brake Technology, a Guide to Precision Sheet Metal Bending*, is a product of this ambitious publishing effort, which includes books, periodicals, videotapes, and an on-line data service.

For a catalog of SME publications, call 1-800-733-4763.

*This book is dedicated to my wife, Patricia, for the countless hours she spent proofreading this work, which would not have been possible without her. Thank you!*

# Contents

# PREFACE

In the 20 odd years that I have been in the precision sheet metal trade, I have never found any comprehensive information regarding press brake operations.

Sure, there were sales brochures and an occasional magazine article, but never could I find a complete text. That void gave me the motivation to write this book.

Over the years I collected and saved every bit of information I found on the subject of press brakes. That, coupled with 20 plus years of experience, gave me the knowledge I try to impart here. I truly hope this work becomes the comprehensive text for press brake operators of the future, as well as those who work in the field today.

Many different people and organizations over the last 100 years have developed the information that I present in this text. To them I am truly indebted. I also thank Larry Binstock and SME who took a chance on me and published this work.

Thank you all.

Steve D. Benson
Salem, Oregon

# Chapter 1

# THE MACHINE

## THE HISTORY AND THE MACHINES

The discovery of metal some 6,000 years before Christ was one of the greatest achievements of ancient times—easily equal in importance to the invention of the wheel. Over the following 2,000 years, people learned to smelt various ores, releasing the elements inside. Archaeological digs have produced many examples of hammered lead and copper from this time period, with sites found from ancient Greece to southern Turkey.

Soon, the newly discovered art of smelting spread throughout the Middle East, allowing metalsmiths to create new alloys such as bronze, a mix of copper and tin. Iron soon joined bronze in the metalsmith's catalog. The discovery and evolution of smelting took place over a 500-year time frame, approximately 1500 B.C. to 1000 B.C., according to records of the time.

Makers of weapons, tools, and ritual objects found many ways to take advantage of metal's practical aspects. They liked its ability to hold a sharp edge, its strengths, and, of course, its durability, not to mention its luster and decorative qualities. These early metalworkers (smiths) were experts at their crafts and technologies. The jewelry, weapons, and coins of the past attest to their level of skill.

In the early part of the 18th century, the art of metallurgy ensured the industrial revolution. Developments in modern chemistry brought about a new and easier method of creating steel. A process developed by Benjamin Huntsman, coupled with Henry Bessemer's economical method of producing wrought iron, became the milestone of the early 18th century and the industrial age.

The late 18th century saw the advent of rolling mills and the beginnings of modern sheet metal. However, it was still crude in both quality and consistency. By the middle of the 19th century there had been enough improvement in both metallurgy and metalworking that a reasonable amount of accuracy could be expected.

Only in the later part of the 20th century did high-tech, computerized precision equipment become available. Today, metalworking is no longer a profession requiring only a strong back. Instead it requires very skilled, highly trained operators to get the most from a new generation of machines.

Methods today range from the old primitive lead strap and mold, now most commonly used by artisans, to newer methods such as straight-line forming, stamping and hydraforming. This book will deal only with straight-line forming, which varies from other types of bending or stamping in that curves and continuous complex bends are not capable of being produced. With straight-line forming, the radius and bend angle may vary greatly even across a single bend, but nothing like an *S* shape is possible. Therefore, we will only be concerned with the press brake, the machine developed for straight-line bending.

At this time there are four different types or styles of press brakes:

- leaf;
- mechanical;
- hydramechanical; and
- hydraulic (down acting, up acting).

Obviously there are vast differences between these various configurations of metalworking equipment. As with most things, the type of machine you use depends on the application, accuracy needed, rates of production, and repeatability. Of course, each machine has its particular advantages, but good machines are available in all five categories. It is not the intention of this book to promote any type of press brake, but simply to explain the abilities and disadvantages of each.

## The Leaf Brake

In most shops, the leaf brake (Figure 1-1) is usually small and manually operated, although many larger ones are now hydraulic. Some even come with very sophisticated CNC (computer numerical control) controllers. Because of its design, the leaf brake is basically limited for use with the lighter gages of sheet metal, 16 gage (0.062 in. [1.58 mm]) or less. It is capable of producing most types and configurations of bend.

The machine itself consists of the main housing, forming bar, front leaf assembly, and clamping mechanism. Each of these will be discussed, including the tooling since it differs in many ways from that of a standard press brake "punch and die set."

### The main housing

The main housing is manufactured out of cast iron because of its durability and strength. There is a large flat area machined into the main body of the casting, along with the working and mounting hardware. This large flat working face is referred to as the platen or bed.

### The forming bar

Attached to the main casting and parallel to the platen is the forming bar or clamping beam, which raises or lowers with a cam or hydraulic cylinders. The forming bar is also where the tooling is attached to the leaf brake. This tooling, incorporated into the process by establishing a bend line, works as the clamp that holds the workpiece in place during the forming process.

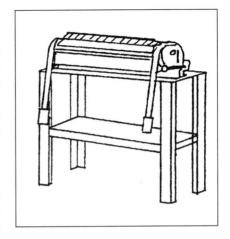

*Figure 1-1. The leaf brake.*

### The tooling

The tooling for a leaf brake is called a "finger" (Figure 1-2) and, like most tooling, it comes in pre-cut widths. The widths normally vary in size to achieve combinations that create box or pan formations. These tools usually have a very small radius as the final inside bend radius is achieved by changing the relationship between the punch, the clamp, and the forming bar.

### The leaf bar

Attached to the main casting is the leaf bar or folding beam. Mounted parallel to the forming bar, the leaf bar performs the actual bending operation by being raised up to an adjustable pre-set limiter, allowing a consistent bend angle throughout the forming process.

## The Mechanical Brake

The mechanical press brake (Figure 1-3) uses a flywheel to produce the power, causing motion in the ram. The ram, the moving part of this press brake, is attached to the flywheel by means of mechanical linkage.

While disengaged, the flywheel builds up the inertia that will, when the flywheel is re-engaged, cause the ram to move up and down under full power. This stored inertia is then available to create the tonnage required for the forming process.

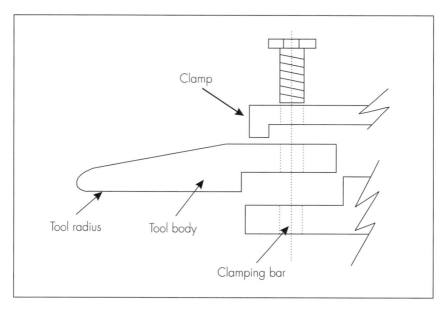

**Figure 1-2.** *Cutaway view of leaf brake tooling and clamping mechanism.*

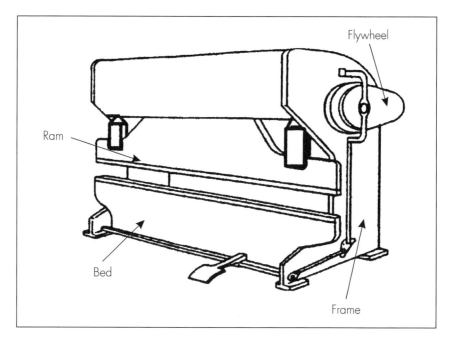

**Figure 1-3.** *Mechanical press brake, with the major machine parts labeled.*

### The bed
The bed is located on top of the bottom plate that holds the bolster, which holds the die in the press brake.

### The ram
The ram is the segment of the press brake that does all the moving. Traditionally, it came downward from above, but the arrival of the up-acting press changed that situation.

The mechanical press brake, still in wide use throughout the sheet metal industry, has the most dangerous design of all types of press brakes. Operators could easily lose fingers or limbs because of drift back in the ram, an inherent fault of a flywheel/clutch design. If operators fail to complete their full machine stroke, the ram could drift back down toward the bed before the clutch assembly completely re-engages, catching the operator, workpieces, or tools in the press brake. The same sort of accidents could happen if the machine's brake is not kept in top working order.

In the hands of a skilled operator, mechanical press brakes can be highly effective. They are, however, no match for the modern hydraulic press brakes for speed, accuracy, or repeatability.

## The Hydramechanical Brake
The hydramechanical press brake's overall design is similar to the mechanical-style press brake. The big difference is in the way the ram is driven. Rather than using a flywheel, a hydraulic pump develops the necessary inertia to drive the ram. This hydraulic pressure causes a hydraulic motor to turn an eccentric shaft, producing the up-and-down action of the ram and the necessary power to produce the bend (Figure 1-4).

Unlike mechanical press brakes that must complete a full stroke of the ram every time, the hydramechanical press brake has the ability to limit its stroke. In other words, you could develop full tonnage at any point along the stroke and then return to the open position. This also allows the open height to be set at any point above the bottom of the stroke. Not only does the hydramechanical press brake offer a vast improvement in

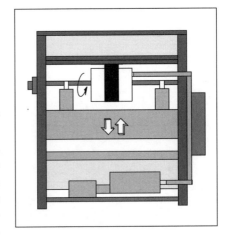

**Figure 1-4.** The hydramechanical press brake uses the rotation of an eccentric shaft to produce the up-and-down motion of the ram.

machine capability and operation over the mechanical brake, but it also offers enchanced safety. Again, compared to the modern hydraulic presses, durability and accuracy of these machines are, for the most part, satisfactory. However, they are no match for the more modern hydraulic press.

In some cases press brakes can be used for heavy-gage materials (Figure 1-5). This brake design, capable of producing large tonnages, is of particular value for coining or heavy forming. As the hydraulic ram is extended, a lever action is created, forcing the ram down. This lever action is how the tonnage of the hydraulic ram is multiplied to create the larger tonnages required by heavy-gage material or for coining. However, accuracy and repeatability are sacrificed for this added power, a flaw inherent in this type of mechanical linkage.

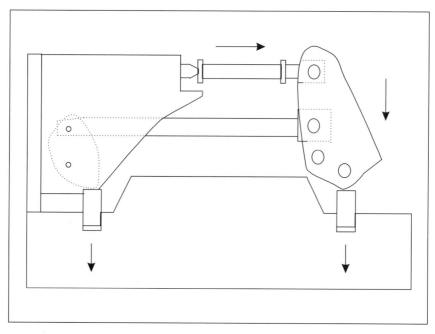

**Figure 1-5.** *This press brake design is capable of producing large tonnages. It uses the in-and-out motion of the drive piston to initiate a lever action, which in turn causes the up-and-down motion of the ram.*

## The Hydraulic Brake

Unlike the hydramechanical press brake that converted the hydraulic energy to mechanical energy with a hydraulic motor fixed to an eccentric shaft, the modern hydraulic press brake uses a hydraulic pump and hydraulic cylinders to move the ram (Figure 1-6). This design is far more efficient, allowing increased speed and accuracy.

The modern hydraulic press brake can be divided into two basic subgroups, up-acting and down-acting (all other types of press brakes are down-acting only).

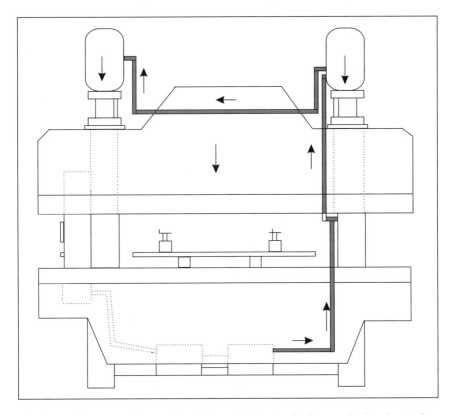

**Figure 1-6.** *The hydraulic press brake forces hydraulic fluid into cylinders (top or bottom) causing the motion in the ram.*

## The up-acting press brake

The French designed, and were the first to use, the up-acting style of press brake. In the author's opinion, up-acting is the best type of press brake, not only because of the ram's guidance and arrangement of rollers, but also because of its natural antideflection characteristics. On this machine you have gravity on your side, working with you instead of against you.

For any mechanical device to have movement, it must have some clearance built in to allow the mechanism to function freely. On the press brake, an important clearance lies between the power source and the ram body. The clearance is just right when the machine is new or rebuilt. However, with age and use this clearance will increase (sometimes dramatically), causing an ever-increasing amount of play in the mechanism. When the press is a down-acting, this excess clearance, or "play," is located on the bottom when no load is present. When a load is applied (see Figure 1-7), such as when a piece of material is formed, this error moves to the top of the connection. This hurts the ram's repeatability, often leading to vast swings in bend angle from one workpiece to the

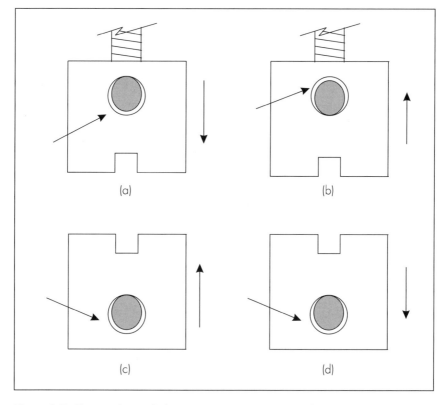

**Figure 1-7.** *The mechanical clearance common to most down-acting press brake linkage (a) being at rest and (b) being under a load; (c) and (d) shows this same clearance as it relates to an up-acting press brake; (c) is shown under a load; and (d) at rest. Note: the clearance shifts on the down-acting and does not shift on the up-acting press.*

next. The up-acting press brake, on the other hand, always keeps this play on the bottom, whether under pressure or not.

### The down-acting press brake

Down-acting hydraulic press brakes represent 90% of all press brakes in use today. Of all the down-acting press brakes, the hydraulic is, by far, the most accurate. These machines are controlled by a CNC or DNC controller (computer numerical control or direct numerical control). The computers, in turn, control a proportional valve system (Figure 1-8). This system allows for ram control in the downward direction, which, in turn, gives accurate bend angle control.

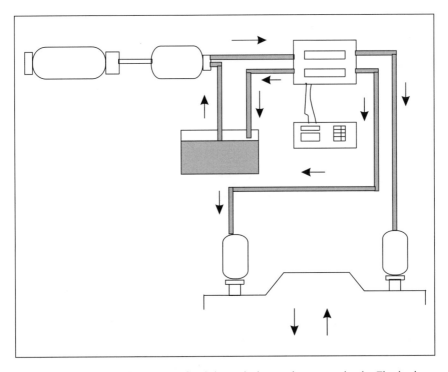

**Figure 1-8.** *The flow of hydraulic fluid through the modern press brake. The hydraulic cylinder is mounted to the ram, removing any need for the bushing and pin joints common in other styles of press brakes. However, with age and wear, cylinders and valving develop variances similar to the error in the pin and bushing style of press brake design.*

# Chapter 2

# TYPES OF BENDS

## THREE TYPES

There are three different types of bending methods used in forming sheet metal: coining, bottom bending, and air forming. Each has a specific purpose and application.

### Coining

Coining (Figure 2-1) was probably the first bending method practiced in the sheet metal trade. The process requires an amount of tonnage so great that the material being formed actually flows. This flowing goes out from the coined segment to that part of the workpiece not under pressure. If the bend radius is sharp (less than 63% of the material thickness), the punch tip can actually penetrate into or past the neutral axis of the bend. There the yield of the material is broken. With this penetration of the neutral axis by the punch tip, the springback almost disappears, and material remains permanently deformed at the point where the pressure was released.

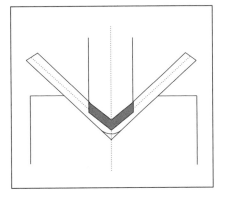

**Figure 2-1.** Coining is a process of springback control in which the punch tip and body actually penetrate the material past the neutral axis under extreme pressure, thus stamping the angle.

In the coining process it is not uncommon to find the tonnage exceeding 50 tons per inch (17,895 kilograms per centimeter) even in light-gage material. Such excessive tonnage requirements make this style of forming impractical for heavier gages of material or for material with high tensile strength. Because of the enormous pressures and the possibility of damage to the tooling or press brake during the process, coining is rarely used today. The only true coining tools still in use are specialty tools such as offset dies, embossing tools, or flatting dies. As a point of note, bottom bending is often referred to as coining, although it is not. These two processes, although similar, are distinct methods of bending.

## Bottom Bending

There are many similarities between coining and bottom bending. With coining, however, the entire surface of the material comes into contact with the tooling, which is stamped so severely that the material actually flows. With bottom bending, on the other hand, only the radius is stamped into the material. As shown in Figure 2-2, there is enough angular tooling clearance between the punch and die to compensate for the springback in the material. Springback is the characteristic of most materials to try to return to the flat position after forming. The angular tooling clearance should be equal to the springback. As pressure is applied to the radius, the material passes by the required angle and up to a total equal to the required angle and the springback; then it is forced back to the required bend angle.

The example shown in Figure 2-2 would be capable of bottoming aluminum or stainless steel, but would overbend a piece of standard cold-rolled steel. Aluminum and stainless steel both have a springback factor of one and one half to two degrees. Cold-rolled steel has approximately

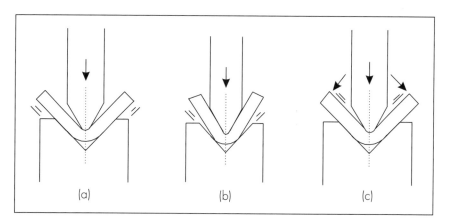

*Figure 2-2.* Bottom bending is similar to coining in that the radius is stamped into the material (a). Springback is controlled through the use of tooling angles (b). The material is brought up to an angle that includes the springback (c) and then is forced back to the die angle.

one half of a degree. Because cold-rolled steel has one half to one degree less than the tooling combination, the bottom bend angle would end up being 91.5 degrees. If you wanted to bottom a bend to 90 degrees in cold-rolled steel, you would need a punch of 90 degrees or 89.5 degrees used in conjunction with a 90-degree bottom die. Again this would allow you to pass 90 degrees to 90.5 degrees and then force the radius back to 90 degrees.

Punch and die relationships vary with different material types than those just discussed, but the idea still works in the same way.

Bottom bending offers consistency in holding a bend angle with far less tonnage than coining. However, this type of forming requires a highly skilled operator, since the tonnages required could damage the workpiece, tooling, or press brake.

### Air Forming

Air forming is a three-point bending operation. The three points are the punch tip and both top corners of the die, as shown in Figure 2-3. Air forming uses the penetration of the punch tip into the die space as the determining factor in achieving the required bend angle. Because its tonnages are greatly reduced from those required for coining or bottoming, air forming is fast becoming the method of choice by most manufacturers. Wear and tear on the press brake and tooling is greatly reduced, leading to a marked increase in equipment longevity.

Air forming is one of the more practical methods of forming in the modern sheet metal shop. One of its biggest advantages is that non-specific tooling can be used. The inside radius (Ir) is arrived at by the width of the die. It can be changed simply by increasing or decreasing the die width. This allows a much wider range of tooling for the operator to use in arriving at the finished product, adjusting errors in layout, or punching in the flat blanked piece.

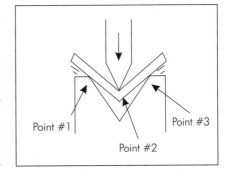

**Figure 2-3.** *Air forming is a three-point method of forming where springback is compensated for by overbending the workpiece by an amount equal to the springback. The radius is allowed to find its natural size.*

As the die width changes, the bend radius changes. And as the radius changes, the bend deduction (BD) changes. Changes in BD are in direct proportion to the Ir.

Although air forming is becoming the most popular method of press brake forming, it does not suit such older styles of press brakes as mechanical or hydramechanical, mainly because of the mechanism's inherent error, as was shown in Figure 1-7. Any change in material thickness or tensile strength during a run of parts would immediately show up as angular variations. Smaller workpieces must lift the ram before encountering the actual machine thrust at the end of the excess clearance. This excess clearance increases the probability of problems.

## Summary

Each of the three foregoing styles of metal forming has a purpose. Each is capable, within its limitations, of producing an excellent product. It takes the practiced eye of the journeyman to know why and when specific techniques should be used.

# Chapter 3

# TOOLS OF THE TRADE

## PRECISION TOOLS OF SHEET METAL

Before being able to operate a press brake in an efficient manner, you need to know the different types of hand tools, their purposes, and correct applications for each. This chapter will discuss only precision tools that apply to the sheet metal trade.

### Square Blades and Rulers

Square blades and rulers are common to many different industries. A woodshop needs rulers and square blades with fractional scales, while in the precision sheet metal trade, a decimal scale is the required norm. Figure 3-1 shows part of an R16 decimal scale. Each inch is divided into 10 equal graduations or "tenths" equal to 0.100 in. between the larger

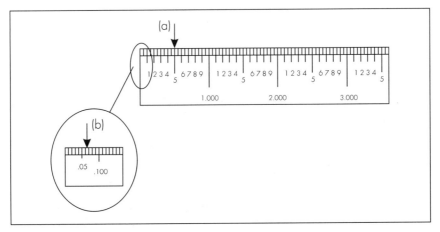

**Figure 3-1.** Common R16 ruler with a scale graduation of (a) tenths, (b) hundredths, and an example estimation of thousandths.

line. These lines are usually marked by a corresponding number (e.g., five tenths or 0.500) (see Figure 3-1a). Between each of these numbered lines are 9 additional equal graduations or "hundredths," each line having a value of 0.010 between them.

Because of the small distances between the lines required of the next graduation down, "thousandths," the lines would become just a blur without the aid of some kind of magnifying glass, and are usually omitted from most scales. It is, however, relatively easy to estimate thousandths; for example, between 0.06 and 0.07 (Figure 3-1b) is 0.065.

While the ruler and square blade stand on their own, the square blade becomes a much more capable hand tool in conjunction with a square or protractor head. Figure 3-2 shows one of several ways to measure a finished workpiece. Figure 3-2a shows a 45-degree bend in a piece of 0.059-in. (1.5-mm) thick material with a 0.06 inch inside bend radius. This workpiece is dimensioned to the outside apex of the bend, 1 in. (25.4 mm) in both directions. To measure this bend to the apex, set your square at 1 in. (25.4 mm), as shown in Figure 3-2b. Then, holding the square

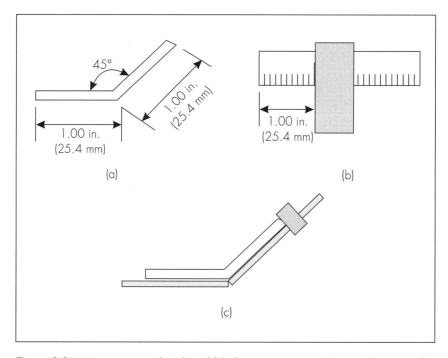

*Figure 3-2.* Using a square head and blade to measure to the outside apex of a bend.

blade flush to the workpiece, take another blade or straight edge and slide it up edge to edge (see Figure 3-2c). If you measured correctly, the sliding blade should meet the set square blade, point to point, at the bottom edge of the square blade apex.

Using the same 1 in. × 1 in. (25.4 mm × 25.4 mm) workpiece with a 45-degree bend, look at how to measure to the inside of the workpiece. By taking the inside shift (ISS) away from the outside dimension, the inside measurement is found.

| | |
|---|---|
| 1.000 in. (25.4 mm) | flange dimension |
| −0.014 in. (0.356 mm) | less inside shift |
| 0.986 in. (25.044 mm) | inside measurable dimension at bend line |

Then just set the square or caliper to 0.986 in. (25.044 mm) and measure to the center of the bend line (Figure 3-3). The third way that the square set can be used is to set the blade 1 in. (25.4 mm) longer than the required dimension. By doing this, you can directly read any error, plus or minus. In the example shown in Figure 3-4 the edge of the workpiece should just cover the 1.000 in. (25.4 mm) mark if the measurement is correct. The examples illustrated in Figures 3-2, 3-3, and 3-4 are by no means the only ways the square set can be used.

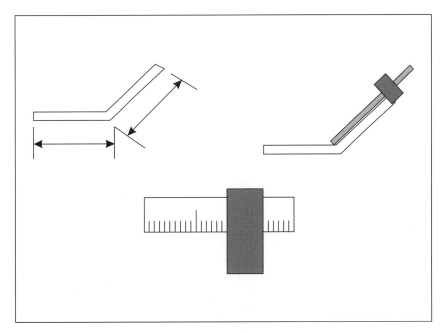

*Figure 3-3.* Using a square head and blade or caliper to measure to the bend.

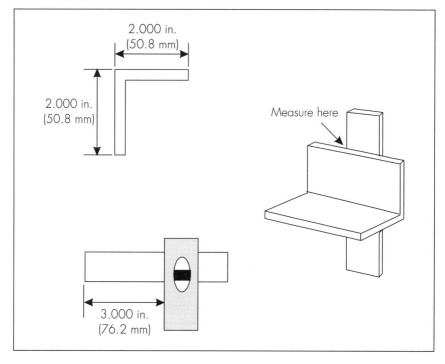

**Figure 3-4.** *With the square blade set to 1 in. (25.4 mm) longer than the measured surface, you can read any dimensional error, plus or minus.*

## Calipers

Three different styles of calipers are in use today (Figure 3-5): vernier, dial, and digital. All are more than adequate for use in the precision sheet metal shop. However, some (such as the vernier caliper) require a practiced eye to read them well.

### The vernier calipers

In the vernier scale shown in Figure 3-6, the upper scale is divided into inch increments. The bottom scale is graduated from 0 to 50, each with a value of 0.050 of an inch. In Figure 3-6a the bottom scale's zero rests somewhere between 0.800 and 0.850 inches. Reading first from the top scale, from left to right, look for the bottom scale's zero. Then read from right to left, in the bottom scale.

Following up the scale, search for the place where the lines on both scales form one single line across the width of both scales. In Figure 3-6a these lines meet on the bottom scale at 0.009. Finding the total measurement just becomes a matter of addition: 0.800 + 0.009 = 0.809. Figure 3-6b shows a dimension of 1.786. Figure 3-6c is 0.954.

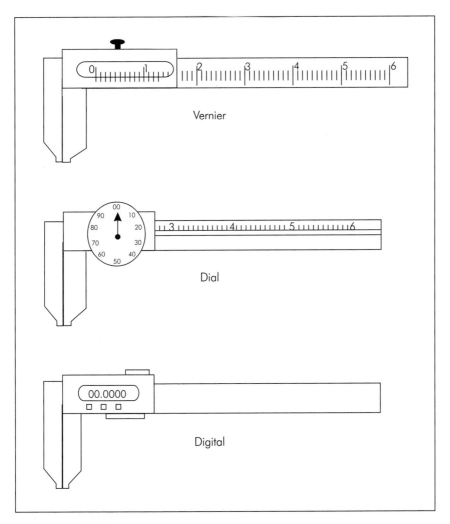

**Figure 3-5.** *Types of calipers.*

### Dial calipers

Dial calipers are read directly from the inch/tenths scale on the caliper's main body; then they are read from the dial for the thousandths dimension.

### Digital calipers

Digital calipers can be read instantaneously from an LCD screen in the caliper head. These, depending on the brand, will even measure to ten-thousandths of an inch.

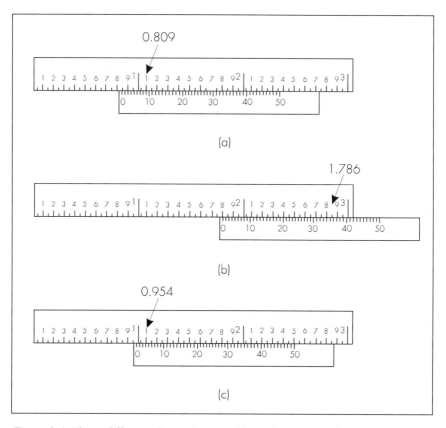

**Figure 3-6.** Three different dimensions and how they are read on an actual vernier scale.

Calipers, more than most tools, must be cleaned and adjusted regularly to maintain their accuracy. Dial calipers need to have the track brushed out daily to keep the gears from jumping a tooth. Vernier and digital calipers only need to be wiped off and adjusted.

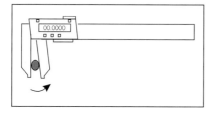

**Figure 3-7.** Making sure that the jaws of the caliper remain parallel is necessary for accurate measurements.

The most important adjustment is done to the jaws, to keep them both parallel. The looseness of the sliding jaw must be kept to a minimum. In Figure 3-7 adjustments and possible error relationships are shown that are common to all three styles of caliper. These items should be checked before each use.

Most brands of calipers can measure more than just the primary jaws. Figure 3-8 shows the different places on the caliper where various measurements can be made. The "stinger" that comes out the end is used to measure depths. Sometimes depth measurements can be made behind the main caliper's body. The inside dimension jaws, located above the main jaws (not shown in the figure), can measure center to center, between holes, or the inside dimensions between the flanges of a workpiece.

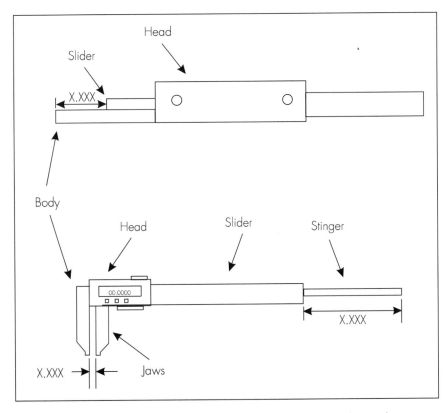

**Figure 3-8.** *Some places on the caliper where measurements can be made.*

## Protractors

Two types of protractors are used in modern sheet metal shops. There is the regular everyday protractor that reads in one-degree increments that can be found in most hardware stores. Also, there is the vernier scale protractor, which works in the same manner as vernier calipers. This style of protractor will read to increments of five-minute accuracy. Figure 3-9 shows both types.

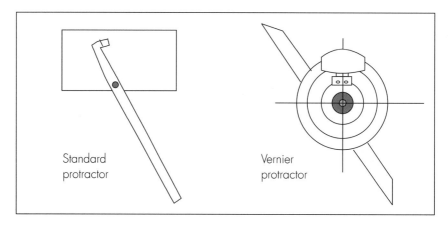

**Figure 3-9.** *Both types of protractors.*

The vernier protractor reads from left or right, from zero to 90 degrees on the outer scale. On the inner scale the increments read from the right or left, from zero to 60 minutes. All measurements are read from the vernier scale (inner). In Figure 3-10 the reading shown would

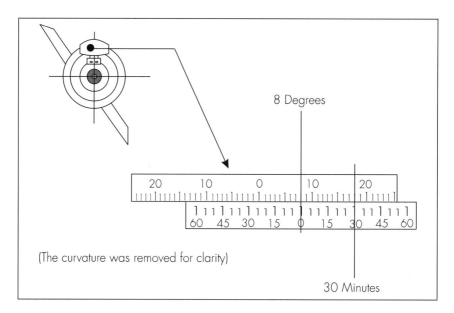

**Figure 3-10.** *The correct way to read a vernier protractor scale.*

be 8 degrees and 30 minutes. This measurement (as with most protractors) reads what's called in the trade the complementary angle instead of the included angle of the bend. In Figure 3-11 the difference between the complementary and included angles are shown.

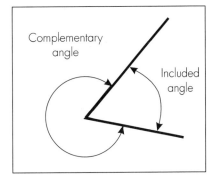

Figure 3-11. Angle callouts.

### Radius Gages

Tools that measure the radius of the workpiece are called radius gages, and normally come in complete sets of standard English or metric sizes. These tools can be used to measure the radius of the punch, the final bend radius (internal or external), or even 90-degree bend angles. Figure 3-12 shows the three most important uses for the radius gage.

If the radius gage can be seated in the same manner as the illustration on the left in Figure 3-12, all bend functions that have been calculated will be correct and true. If the radius of the workpiece is different than the punch (air forming), you will be able to calculate the numbers for the new inside radius.

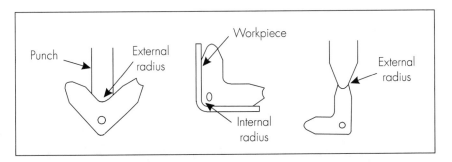

Figure 3-12. Several ways to use the radius gage for the manufacture of any sheet metal part.

# Chapter 4

# THE CONTROLLERS

All types of controllers have the same basic functions, including the calculation of ram depth, backgage origin, and flange lengths. Do not give too much meaning to the way that one manufacturer or another labels things. An "end dimension" is an end dimension, and a flange is a flange, no matter what a specific manufacturer may call them.

## THE MODES

There are two different modes in which you can operate most controllers, depth mode, and angle mode. Depth mode can best be described as the manual operation of the press brake with only a minimum of computer control. On the other hand, angle mode can be characterized as the relinquishment of most control functions to the computer. Skilled operators will argue as to which is the better way, but it comes down to which method makes an operator feel most comfortable.

There are a few things the two methods have in common.

### Setting the Backgage

In both methods, all parameters need to be set before anything else can be done. In understanding how the backgage is calibrated, look at it in the same way the computer sees it. Figure 4-1 shows both human and computer points of view. Humans see the backgage as sitting at the 4.000-in. (101.6-mm) position, with the zero being located at the center of the die set. The computer sees the die set as 4.000 in. and the backgage location as zero. Most modern press brakes use 4.000 in. as the zero point.

When the backgage origin button is pushed, the backgage finds what it considers to be zero (4.000 in. [101.6 mm]). At that point you can input the required backgage dimensions for the program being readied. A dimension input into the controller is automatically adjusted to the computer's point of view (Figure 4-2). If you tell the controller to move the backgage to the 3.000-in. (76.2-mm) position, the backgage would find what it sees as 1.000 in. (25.4 mm).

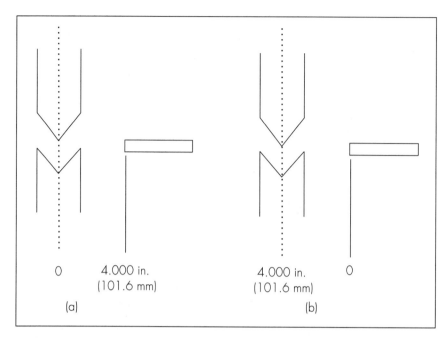

**Figure 4-1.** Your view of zero (a), and the computer's view (b).

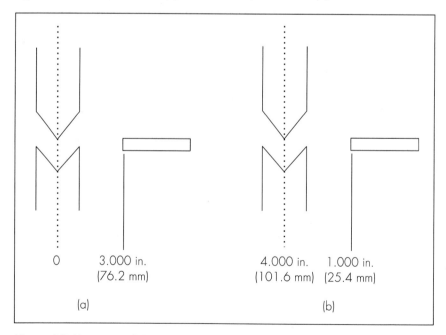

**Figure 4-2.** Your view of 3 in. (76.2 mm) (a), and the computer's view (b).

There is a good reason to pay close attention to how the controller sees things. For instance, it may become necessary to adjust the backgage position parameters to reflect a true and valid location. To make the backgage move closer to the die set you would input a positive number; to move the backgage away you would input a negative number. For example, if you bent a part and it measured 4.010 in. (101.854 mm) instead of the required 4.000 in. (101.6 mm), and all other bends were larger by 0.010 in. (0.254 mm), you would need to input +0.010 in. into the backgage parameters and then press the origin button to re-zero the backgage to the required location.

For the older variety of backgage, or for those people who do not use precision ground tooling, there is a slightly different method by which the 4.000-in. (101.6-mm) backgage location is found. With standard nonprecision ground tooling, each tooling change results in a change in die set location. Because the center of the tooling moves in relationship to the backgage, the backgage reference point will need to move directly to match. This is accomplished with a calibration block. Two gage blocks are centered in the tooling under slight pressure, one at either end of the punch and die set. The backgage beam is then loosened from its holder and slid up to a gage block. Extra care needs to be taken to ensure squareness to the tooling. Apply only light, equal pressure. When the beam is clamped into position and the gage blocks are removed, the backgage is calibrated. Figure 4-3 shows a typical gage block calibration.

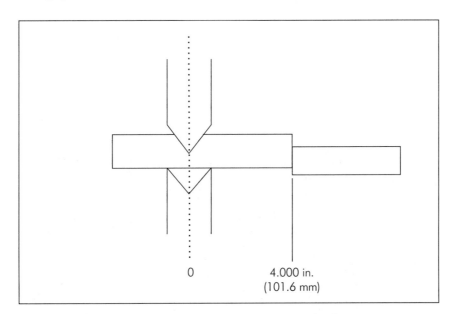

**Figure 4-3.** The gage block is used to calibrate non-CNC backgages.

## Moving the Reference Point

Every type or brand of controller needs periodic adjustments to the backgage zero location. The need for adjustment could result from an odd tooling center or the part pulling into the die wrong. To make this type of adjustment on most machines, you need to enter data changes in computer terms. For example, if the backgage must be moved out 0.050 in. (1.27 mm), you must tell the controller to move 0.050 in. in a negative direction. Remember, the computer sees things the opposite of you (Figure 4-4).

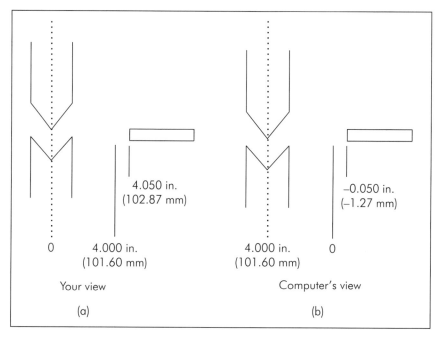

**Figure 4-4.** *Human view (a) and computer view (b) of an adjustment.*

## Parameter Adjustments

From time to time dual motor machines need to be brought into or taken out of square. The object is to obtain the same physical location on both the right and left sides. To do this, start the press and controller empty, with parameters set back to the factory specifications. Factory parameters are usually written inside the controller cabinet. Once the machine has been zeroed, install tooling on both sides of the press brake bed. Bend test pieces, one on either side. Next adjust the parameters so the test pieces measure the same on both sides. Remember, the data will need to be changed into computer terms.

## Depth origin

The depth origin is set two different ways, depending on the machine. Normally, you set the depth to an amount equal to or greater than the material thickness (Mt.). This ensures that you will not lock up the ram or break the tooling on the first hit. From there the ram is adjusted up or down by hand to achieve the required angle. The single-axis press brake, having no controllers, is set manually, with the bottom of the stroke being the depth origin.

## Depth axis

Setting the depth axis in a computer-controlled machine is a simple task. Figure 4-5 shows the tooling under increasing pressure from contact of the punch and die faces. This predetermined pressure is set by the manufacturer and is a common zero point of the controller and the tooling. It allows every operator to find the same reference point, regardless of the program being run or the machine being used.

Sometimes you will come across pieces of tooling that are too small to withstand the pressure of zeroing. This is why you must begin with enough tooling to achieve the required tonnage of zeroing. Keep in mind that the excess tooling can always be removed. In most cases, a 4-in. (101.6-mm) piece of tooling will be enough to handle the pressure. This provides a consistent method that will make setups faster and easier because there is the same depth of punch penetration from flange to flange or part to part. If a tooling combination has a maximum allowable tonnage of a half ton (6.9 kPa), but the press requires four tons (55 kPa) to zero, extra tooling must be added to allow the additional tonnage required (Figure 4-6).

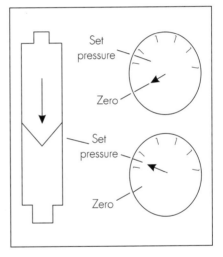

**Figure 4-5.** Zeroing the press brake's ram.

## Programs

Programs consist of at least one step, with every step divided into substeps containing the pertinent information concerning each bend.

Imagine a tray that represents the overall program and four smaller trays that represent each step. Now take the first of the small trays and

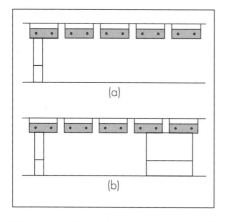

**Figure 4-6.** *Always be sure to use enough tooling to handle the required tonnage for zeroing. If the amount of tooling cannot handle four tons (55 kPa) of pressure (a), enough tooling must be added to handle the tonnage and balance the load across the width of the machine (b).*

put all of the information for bend number one in it. Repeat this process as many times as there are bends. When the four small trays are all placed in the large tray, the program is completed. The process is illustrated in Figure 4-7.

If, after running the first setup piece, you find the flanges off by 0.100 in. (2.54 mm), there are two ways to correct this program. You can change each step by 0.100 in. or just move the backgage's reference point. It is only necessary to change the machine's zero point plus or minus an amount equal to the error.

## Depth Mode

In depth mode the controller requires very few pieces of information. First, the depth of penetration must be input. This is the distance from zero to where the ram stops. In general, 1.25 times the material thickness is the best place to start for a 90-degree bend in a 6-in. (152.4 mm) piece of cold-rolled steel. For example, a 6-in. material piece with a thickness of 0.060 in. (1.52 mm) would have a depth of 0.075 in. (1.91 mm) to 0.085 in. (2.16 mm), assuming you are air forming. This number goes up or down in relationship to the bend length.

Running a CNC controller in depth mode is similar to running an older style, non-CNC press brake, but you have the advantage of multiple steps, extreme accuracy, and the repeatability of a CNC control.

### The flange function

When running in depth mode there are two different ways to input flange length data (how deep the backgage is set). First, input the outside dimension of the bend and then use the bend allowance step to compensate. Or, calculate the location of the bend line and input that as the backgage location.

### Bend allowance function

To adjust for changes in the material that occur during the bending process, a controller's bend allowance is used. It will compensate for the changes in material by adjusting a dimension. A bend allowance used in

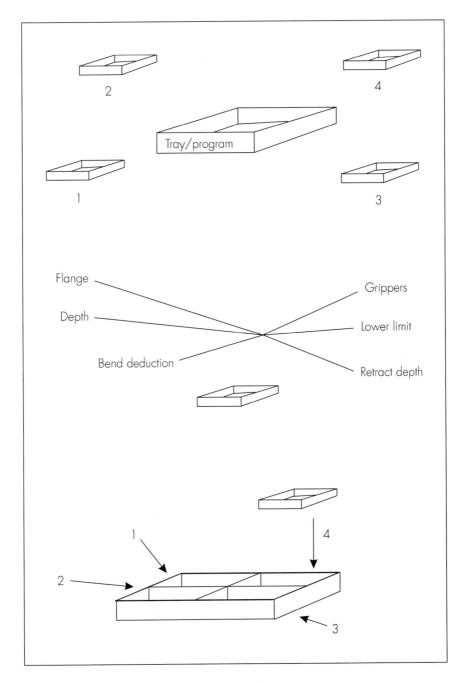

**Figure 4-7.** Programming is like having a series of trays that fit inside each other, building ultimately into a completed program for many small pieces.

calculating bend deductions is not the same as the bend allowance used on most controllers. A controller's bend allowance is equal to one half of a bend deduction.

## Crossover functions

The next level of controller functions are crossover functions, that work in either depth or angle mode. The first of these finds the gripper height. This is the location where the actual stop sits. Most modern controllers offer from three to nine positions. In addition to three standard positions, six are variations of "flip up, move to position, gage drop into place." These are used to maintain a stop position in relation to the tooling. Some of the older or less sophisticated controllers will not have this function. The machine stops are raised or lowered by means of a hand screw. Note: major adjustments on advanced CNC machines are also adjusted by hand and then fine tuned by the controller.

## Retract depth function

Retract depth or "pinch point" are the same thing—the point where the punch first grabs the material just hard enough to hold it against the top of the die. This function holds the workpiece, while the backgage retracts out of the way. Retract length is the distance the backgage moves out of the way of the part being formed. Retract depth allows a reverse flange bend to pass. A reverse flange bend is one where the first bend is bent down in relation to the second bend. Without the retract depth function, a reverse flange would cause the first bend to swing up into the backgage as the second bend is completed.

## Lower limit function

The lower limit controls how far open the press will come from the zero depth. It allows different sized flanges to pass when being removed or moved to the next position. This open height makes the press more efficient as well as safer to operate. Because the machine needs to be opened only far enough for the part to pass, the chance of a body part being included in the bend is greatly reduced.

## Slow bend speed function

Slow bend speed is the rate that the ram actually pushes the material into the die space. This is not a required function in either mode, but its uses are many. It is used mostly where back bending occurs or where the operator needs more delicate control than is possible by hand. The slow bend position is the point in the ram's approach when slow bend speed is activated.

## Angle Mode

The best way to describe angle mode is to say that it allows the controller to assume complete control over the operation of the press brake, including calculating of all the bend data and the physical operations. While running the press brake, there is little for the operator to do but hand material to the machine. However, it still requires a skilled operator to find punching and correct for material changes. As good as the CNC is at controlling the machine, it cannot select the correct tooling or write the programs.

## TERMINOLOGY

The following function terms vary from controller to controller. You may need to consult the operator's manual for a specific machine.

**Angle function.** The angle data is used to calculate the final bend angle you wish to achieve after forming. The tricky part is that the angle input to the controller is what's also called in the trade the complementary angle, as measured on the outside. The angle input into the controller will be 180 degrees minus the bend angle. For example, a 45-degree bend would be input as 135 degrees; a 92–degree bend would be 88 degrees. From this the controller computes the decimal depth that the ram needs to achieve. When the operator steps on the pedal, the ram will go to the depth calculated. Most controllers have an angle adjust step. In angle mode the adjust step needs its value in degrees. This will normally be input as a direct + or – decimal degree to move the ram up or down.

**Bend length function.** For the controller to calculate how much pressure/depth is required, several pieces of information are necessary. One is the length of the material to be formed. This is the total extent of tooling that comes in contact with the workpiece.

**Die width function.** The die width is one more required piece of information used in the depth calculations. This is the distance across the vee opening. It is necessary to compute the necessary tonnage.

**Punch radius function.** On the tip of the punch is a radius, which the controller needs to know for its bending computations. A unique rule applies to this controller function. The input will not only depend on the punch tip's radius, but also on whether or not it is a sharp bend. If the punch radius is sharp in relation to the material thickness, the sharp bend value is used for the controller to perform most efficiently.

**Die radius function.** On both of the top two edges of the vee die opening is a radius, which varies from 0.008 in. (0.203 mm) to at least

0.125 in. (3.175 mm). This radius must be incorporated for the controller to accurately compute the required data. The sharper this radius, the greater the amount of drag on the material as it is drawn into the die space. Each radius has a place and a purpose in the forming process. The controller just needs to know what you have selected.

**Die angle function.** The included die angle is selected on the basis of springback in the material. Springback, a property of the material that allows it to return to its original shape, varies from one material to the next. The greater the springback, the smaller the included die angle. Die angle is used to increase the amount of punch clearance required to bend the workpiece up to and past the finished bend angle. The controller needs to know the die angle to complete the mathematics necessary to run a part.

# Chapter 5

# SAFETY TIPS

Like any other manufacturing apparatus, press brakes can be dangerous unless appropriate caution is taken during, and even before, operation. Before proceeding with other elements of press brakes, it is prudent to take a brief look at some safety pitfalls that could put press brake operators in jeopardy.

## MACHINE SETUP

Before any tooling is installed, the ram must be locked in the "shut height" position. Once the press is locked in a position where the ram can no longer close any tighter, the tooling can slide safely into the press. It may take several tries to achieve the proper gap between the ram and the bed, which must open far enough for easy installation but not so much as to allow the tooling to fall out (Figure 5-1).

Not all tooling can be loaded universally into the press brake. Some can be loaded correctly only one way. The best way to know if you are installing the tooling correctly is to look at the tooling from the end view

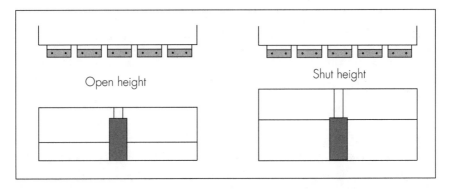

**Figure 5-1.** Open and shut heights regulate ram travel. When tooling is installed, the ram must be locked in the shut height position as a safety precaution.

and check the flow of power. Figure 5-2 shows a standard precision ground tooling set.

Before installing any tooling, check for previous damage that may cause trouble. Then clean both the machine and tools. Check to make sure the tooling angles match correctly for the type of forming being attempted (Figure 5-3). Special care needs to be taken to ensure that the total applied tonnage does not exceed the abilities of the tooling.

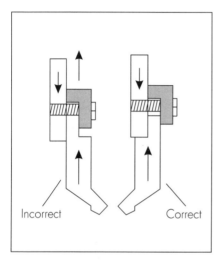

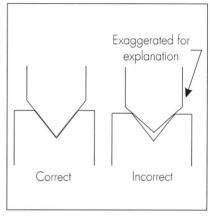

**Figure 5-3.** *Tooling angles can be badly mismatched. Operators must check to be certain that angles match the type of forming being attempted.*

**Figure 5-2.** *The unit on the left is incorrectly installed and could damage the press brake as well as cause serious bodily injury.*

## OPERATIONAL SAFETY

When two or more operators can reach point of operation hazards, all of them must have their own controls and some sort of point-of-operation safeguards. However, when only one person can reach the controls, only one must be considered the operator. This duty should never be shared. The operator should always be the one to make sure that his or her co-worker is clear of the press before the bending process begins.

Will the stops flip out of the way in time? Will the ram come open far enough to get the formed piece out of the press? Is the backgage going to crash into the tooling? These questions can be answered in a dry run of the program and press, which must be performed before any job is started.

## Caution Near the Press

Never apply any pressure against the backgage. Only a light touch is necessary to produce a good part. Pushing against the backgage with unnecessary force puts the operator in the position of "leaning" into the machine; one slip and the operator can fall into it. It also is an inconsistent method, as you cannot push under pressure equally time and time again.

Caution should always be used when reaching behind the tooling. Make sure the backgage is in position, locked, before hands are placed anywhere near the tooling.

### Flywheel press brakes

When you operate a flywheel-driven mechanical press brake, extreme attention needs to be paid to drift. If the ram is not brought back up to or past top dead center, there is a good chance that the ram will drift back down the wrong way before the clutch re-engages. Not knowing where the ram is in relation to the stroke is the single most common reason for loss of fingers and limbs.

*Remember, with a flywheel-driven press brake there is no way to reverse the stroke. If you are caught, the stroke has to be completed!* Please look closely at Figure 5-4.

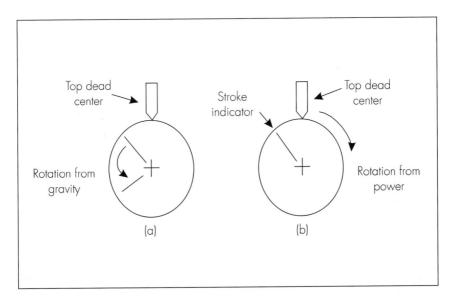

**Figure 5-4.** *The flywheel-driven mechanical press brake is the most dangerous of all press brakes. The operator must not stop the rotation of the ram (a) before the press has passed top dead center (b).*

## GENERAL SAFETY TIPS

Here are some general safety tips for operating press brakes (see Figure 5-5).

- *Never* put any part of your body between the punch and die.
- *Never* let your fingers or body parts come between your workpiece and the machine.
- *Never* hold your workpiece over the top of a previous bend.
- *Never* place your face and upper body in the way of workpiece movement.
- *Never* sit in front of the press brake, as you may not be able to move out of the way quickly enough in an emergency.
- *Never* interrupt someone or allow yourself to be interrupted when operating a press brake.

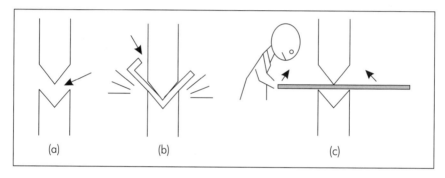

**Figure 5-5.** *Never put any part of your body between the punch and die or let your fingers or body parts come between your workpiece and the machine (a). Never hold your workpiece over the top of a previous bend (b). Keep your face and upper body out of the way of workpiece movement, so you don't get slapped (c).*

### Safety Law, Training, and Shop Rules

Training in how to operate press brakes in conformity with the law is an absolute necessity for all pressroom employees. Formal rule booklets should be developed, thoroughly explaining how to *safely* perform all pressroom tasks. Such booklets should be based on U.S. OSHA, laws from the applicable state, company rules, and, certainly, ANSI B11.3 1982 (R-1994). Included should be the eight options for point-of-operation safeguarding (see Figure 5-6) explained in ANSI's B11.3 booklet, "Safety Requirements for Construction, Care, and Use of Power Brakes." Supervisors, lead persons, and the engineering department should contribute input and review the booklet before the rules are finalized. If the workers are represented by a labor union, the officers should have an opportunity to participate in the process. Once the rule booklet is finalized, all employees should be periodically instructed in each item. Proper maintenance procedures must be followed as specified in the machine manufacturers' own operation and maintenance manuals. Proper maintenance procedures are a key part of press brake safety. Remember, safety is a state of mind, and everyone in the organization must follow and support safe procedures.

1. *Presence sensing device—light curtain or radio frequency*

   Control reliability, brake monitoring and safety distance. Two-hand or foot operation. Sides guarded? Protection required on down stroke only (device can be muted on up stroke). Options: stop at TDC or make full stroke starting above workpiece or two-hand control to auto-stop at 1/4 in. (6.4 mm)—then foot switch to finish stroke (fast approach—slow bend—fast return).

2. *Two-hand control*

   Control reliability, brake monitoring—safety distance. Option: two-hand control on down stroke only and foot through balance of stroke.

3. *Pullback (pull-out)*

   Two-hand or foot operation.

4. *Restraint (hold-out)*

   Two-hand or foot operation.

5. *Hostage control*

   Operator control station (hand or foot) permanently located at a safe distance from the point of operation.

6. *Barrier guard*

   Fixed, adjustable, hinged (interlocked?), two-hand or foot—paragraph (c) and table 0-10 of OSHA 1910.217.

7. *Gates, type "B"*

   Control reliability, brake monitoring—two-hand or foot, sides guarded?

8. *Safeguarding by distance*

   Maintaining a safe distance between operator(s) and point of operation, determined by the dimensions of the part being formed (normally used in conjunction with foot operation). Is the operator really protected if they have to hold on to the part with both hands?

NOTE: Hand-feeding tools can be used in conjunction with some of the above devices, but are not recognized as a point of operation device by themselves.

NOTE: Above point of operation safeguarding operations are explained in ANSI's B11.3 booklet entitled "Safety Requirements for the Construction, Care, and Use of Power Press Brakes" (1982 Edition).

**Figure 5-6.** *Point of operation safeguarding.*

# Chapter 6

# GENERAL MATHEMATICS

## INTEGERS

If you are reading this book you most likely have at least a basic understanding of general mathematics. Since there is a fair amount of math involved from this point on, this chapter is to refresh your memory. If you can use the refresher, read on. If not, skip this chapter—and maybe the next.

Our numbering system is called the Arabic system. The system consists of 10 symbols or digits: 0, 1, 2, 3, 4, 5, 6, 7, 8, 9. The value of a number depends on its position. For example, take the following integers:

- 5,000 is read as five thousand;
- 500 is read as five hundred;
- 50 is read as fifty;
- 5 is read as five;
- 05 is read as five;
- 005 is read as five.

A zero placed before a number does not change the value of that number, but a zero placed after the number does change its value. One zero placed after the number increases the value of that number by a factor of 10. Two zeros multiply that same number by 100. With the third zero you would be multiplying by 1,000, and so on.

Numbers are counted from left to right and separated into groups of three by commas. In this way the reading of each number is facilitated.

### Decimals

A decimal point is used to express a value less than one. The value of a number is divided by 10 for each position we move from left to right. Take the following examples:

- 0.3 equals three tenths of one;
- 0.03 equals three hundredths of one;

- 0.003 equals three thousandths of one;
- 0.0003 equals three ten thousandths of one.

With integers, a zero placed before the number does not change its value, but a zero placed after the number does. In decimals, the opposite is true. When computing decimals, the number is divided by 10 as we move from left to right. A zero placed after the digit does nothing to change the value of that number. The following numbers, although written differently, all equal seven hundred one thousandths:

- 0.7;
- 0.70;
- 0.700;
- 0.7000.

Note: When reading an integer together with a decimal, inject the word "and" between the integer and the decimal. The final digit carries the label indicating how the decimal should be read, for example, tenths, hundredths, etc. The decimal 15.352 is read "fifteen and three hundred fifty-two thousandths."

## Addition

Addition is described as the sum of two or more numbers. Negative or positive, each number has an absolute value. When adding numbers of like signs simply find the sum and use the same sign. If the numbers are of different signs, we find the difference between the numbers and use the sign of the greater valued digit. When adding columns of mixed sign numbers, it is easier to add like signs and then combine the two signs.

The following are some examples of each:

| | | | |
|---|---|---|---|
| +5 | −2 | −8 | −2 |
| +3 | −3 | +5 | +6 |
| +8 | −5 | −3 | +4 |

### Addition axiom

The addition axiom states that equal values are given to different variables, the sums will always be equal.

For example, if $a = b$ then $a + 2 = b + 2$. The axiom also may be expressed as the following: if $a = b$ and $c = d$, then $a + c = b + d$.

## Subtraction

Subtraction can be described as the inverse operation of addition. In the subtraction process we are removing one absolute value from that of another.

## Subtraction axiom

If equal quantities are subtracted from the same or equal quantities, the differences are then equal. For example, if $a = b$ then $a - 5 = b - 5$. Therefore the axiom can be stated as the following: if $a = b$ and $c = d$, then $a - c = b - d$.

## Multiplication

Multiplication is the method by which numbers or quantities are added a given number of times. For example, two four times equals $2 + 2 + 2 + 2$; 4 times $a$ equals $a + a + a + a$. Both the commutative and associative properties apply to multiplication. The commutative property is expressed as $3 \times 2$ equals $2 \times 3$; or $ab = ba$. The associative property is stated as $abc = a(bc) = (ab)c$. The distributive property holds over addition and is expressed as $3(a + b)$ equals $3a + 3b$.

## Division

Division is the inverse of multiplication and is the process of determining the number of times that a given number contains another number.

## Division axiom

The division axiom is an axiom of equality. If equal quantities are divided by the same or equal value the quotients are equal. For example, if $a = b$, then $a/4 = b/4$. The axiom therefore can be expressed as: if $a = b$ and $c = d$, then $a/c = b/d$. Note: no number can be divided by zero, it is an undefined operation.

## Order of Operation

In algebraic operations there is a specific order in which calculations are to be performed. This order is defined in the "rules of operation" that follow:

1. If parentheses, powers, or roots are included, these operations are performed before anything else, including multiplication and division, for example (xxx), $x^x$, $\sqrt{\phantom{x}}$.
2. Multiplication and division are always performed next ($\times$ or $*$).
3. Addition and subtraction may be done in any order ($+$ or $-$).

# Chapter 7

# TRIGONOMETRY (RIGHT ANGLE)

There are innumerable ways in which trigonometry is used in manufacturing a finished sheet metal part. However, some are more relevant than others. Trigonometry may be used to find dimensions not given directly on the customer blueprint (Figure 7-1).

Tangents, sines, and degrees of angle are used in solving the bend functions. Some good examples of these functions follow.

The outside setback (OSSB) equals:

Tangent of one half the degree of angle × (Rp. + Mt.)

The inside through the material thickness (ISTM) equals:

Tangent of one half the degree of angle × Mt.

In right angle trigonometry the following is always true (Figure 7-2):

- Angle *c* equals 90 degrees.
- Side *C* equals the largest dimension.
- All angles must add up to 180 degrees.

Note: sides *A* and *B* are of equal value in the case of a right angle triangle also having two 45-degree angles.

With just three pieces of information we can mathematically explain the remainder of any triangle. Two sides and an angle or two angles and a side will work. The formulas in Table 7-1 are for finding missing angles or sides of a right angle triangle. Sides are denoted by upper case letters and angles by lower case letters.

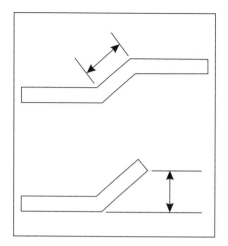

**Figure 7-1.** *Some examples of dimensions that may be missing as direct callouts on the blueprint.*

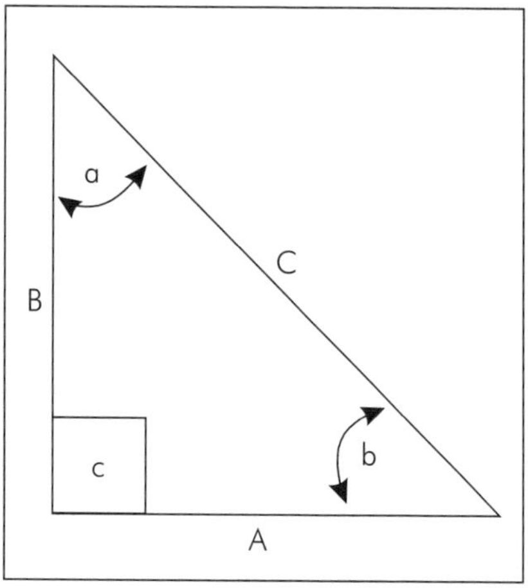

**Figure 7-2.** *Parts of a right triangle.*

## Table 7-1. Formulas for Right Angle Triangle

| *To find the sides:* | *To find the angles:* |
|---|---|
| 1) $C = \sqrt{A^2 + B^2}$ | 1) $a = 90° - b$ |
| 2) $A = \sqrt{C^2 - B^2}$ | 2) $b = 90° - a$ |
| 3) $B = \sqrt{C^2 - A^2}$ | 3) $\sin^{-1} a = A/C$ |
| 4) $C = B/\sin b$ | 4) $\cos^{-1} a = B/C$ |
| 5) $C = B/\cos a$ | 5) $\sin^{-1} b = B/C$ |
| 6) $C = A/\cos b$ | 6) $\cos^{-1} b = A/C$ |
| 7) $C = A/\sin a$ | 7) $\tan^{-1} a = A/B$ |
| 8) $A = B/\tan b$ | 8) $\tan^{-1} b = B/A$ |
| 9) $B = A \tan b$ | 9) $c = 90°$ |
| 10) $A = C \cos b$ | |
| 11) $A = C \sin a$ | |
| 12) $B = C \sin b$ | |
| 13) $B = C \cos a$ | |

Following are some examples of how the formulas for the sides actually work. Included are the three pieces of information required to solve the given triangle.

Angle $c$ = 90 degrees
Angle $b$ = ?
Angle $a$ = 30 degrees
Side $C$ = ?
Side $B$ = 0.750 in. (19.05 mm)
Side $A$ = ?

In any right angle trigonometry problem the total number of degrees of angle must always equal 180 degrees. In any right angle trigonometry problem, angle $c$ will always equal 90 degrees, meaning that angles $b$ and $a$ must also total 90 degrees. In the foregoing example, angle $a$ is known to be 30 degrees; so, by subtracting 30 degrees from 90 degrees we can say that angle $b$ is equal to 60 degrees.

Angle $c$ = 90 degrees
Angle $b$ = 60 degrees
Angle $a$ = 30 degrees
Side $A$ = ?
Side $B$ = 0.750 in. (19.05 mm)
Side $C$ = ?

It is that simple, as long as two of the three pieces of information are angles. How the angles are found when none are given but angle $c$ is covered later in this chapter.

To complete the remainder of this problem, refer back to the list of formulas (Table 7-1) to find the ones that work with the information available. In Figure 7-2 we know that side $B$ is equal to 0.750 in. (19.05 mm). We also know all three angles. Searching down the list of formulas in Table 7-1, from the "to find the sides" column, we need to find a formula that will find side $A$. For now let's use formula number 8:

side $A$ = side $B$/tangent of angle $b$

To begin, your calculator should be in degree mode. Key in the value of angle $b$ or 60 degrees, then press the tangent key. Store this answer in memory. Now key in 0.750 in. (19.05 mm), (side $B$) and divide it by the value in memory. The answer should be 0.433 in. (10.998 mm), the length of side $A$.

Angle $c$ = 90 degrees
Angle $b$ = 60 degrees
Angle $a$ = 30 degrees
Side $C$ = ?
Side $B$ = 0.750 in. (19.05 mm)
Side $A$ = 0.433 in. (10.998 mm)

Now we have five of the six segments; we return to the formula list to repeat the same process as for side $A$.

Searching the list, we need to go no farther than the first formula:

Side $C = \sqrt{(A^2 + B^2)}$

To key this into the calculator, start with 0.750 in. (19.05 mm) followed by the squaring key ($x^2$), and save this sum to memory. Note: it is best to always use the same base numbers and angles to keep from compounding any error. Now key in 0.433 in. (10.998 mm) (side $A$) and square it. This number should be added to the sum in memory and your answer should read 0.749989. Store this figure in memory, just in case.

Taking 0.749989 we will now need to find its square root. With this value keyed up, use the shift key followed by the squaring key ($x^2$). The shift or second function key changes the squaring key into the square root key. The answer should read 0.866 in. (21.996 mm).

The final set of answers to our original problem are the following:

Angle $c$ = 90 degrees
Angle $b$ = 60 degrees
Angle $a$ = 30 degrees
Side $C$ = 0.866 in. (21.996 mm)
Side $B$ = 0.750 in. (19.05 mm)
Side $A$ = 0.433 in. (10.998 mm)

If we already knew the lengths but no angles (angle $c$ is the exception at 90 degrees), we would need to use the other formula list (Table 7-1 "to find the angles"). Using the same triangle from Figure 7-2, let's assume the following problem:

Angle $c$ = 90 degrees
Angle $b$ = ?
Angle $a$ = ?
Side $C$ = 1.900 in. (48.26 mm)
Side $B$ = 1.833 in. (46.56 mm)
Side $A$ = 0.500 in. (12.7 mm)

All that is needed is to find one angle and then subtract that from 90 degrees to get the answer to that third angle. Let's solve for angle $b$ by using the fifth formula:

side $B$/side $C$ = the sine of angle $b$

Using the data, work the formula.

1.833/1.900 = 0.9647368

This number needs to be converted to degrees and minutes. Before we learn to use the calculator to solve the degree/minutes conversion, a brief review of the trigonometry tables is needed. Table 7-2, just one page from the trigonometry tables, is used to solve our second problem.

Each table is labeled with an angle and consists of eight columns both at the top and the bottom. The columns are labeled: M (minutes), sine, cosine, tangent, cotangent, secant and cosecant. Looking up or down the sine columns, we look for 0.9647368, the sine of angle b.

Note: each page has two different angles, smaller on top and larger on the bottom.

Find the closest number to the one that you are looking for. For the current problem, 0.9647368 is about 75 degrees.

Follow the sine column up to find the number that comes the closest to 0.9647368. We find that to be 0.9648. Now follow that line to the outside column, the one marked with an "M," the minutes column.

The "M" columns are located on both sides of the chart. The column on the left reads from the top of the page and the column on the right reads from the bottom. So, in reading across we find that 0.9648 is equal to 75 degrees, 45 minutes.

Angle c = 90 degrees
Angle b = 75 degrees 45 minutes
Angle a = ?
Side C = 1.900 in. (48.26 mm)
Side B = 1.833 in. (46.56 mm)
Side A = 0.500 in. (12.7 mm)

To complete the last part of the current problem, subtract 75 degrees, 45 minutes from 90 degrees; and that would be 14 degrees, 15 minutes. So the answers look like this:

Angle c = 90 degrees
Angle b = 75 degrees 45 minutes
Angle a = 14 degrees 15 minutes
Side C = 1.900 in. (48.26 mm)
Side B = 1.833 in. (46.56 mm)
Side A = 0.500 in. (12.7 mm)

There is an easier way to find the same information using a simple and inexpensive scientific calculator.

Finding angle b, we started with the formula:

side B/side C = the sine of angle b

Side B equals 1.833 in. (46.56 mm) and C equals 1.900 in. (48.26 mm). After dividing 1.833 by 1.900, we found the sine of angle b or 0.9647368. Once the problem is worked to this point, key in "shift-sine" (shift being the same as a second function key). Now the calculator should

# Table 7-2. Trigonometry Table

### 15 Degrees

| M | Sine | Cosine | Tangent | Cotangent | Secant | Cosecant | M |
|---|------|--------|---------|-----------|--------|----------|---|
| 0 | 0.25882 | 0.9659 | 0.27695 | 3.732 | 1.0353 | 3.8637 | 60 |
| 1 | 0.2591 | 0.9658 | 0.26826 | 3.7277 | 1.0353 | 3.8595 | 59 |
| 2 | 0.25938 | 0.9658 | 0.26857 | 3.7234 | 1.0354 | 3.8553 | 58 |
| 3 | 0.25966 | 0.9657 | 0.26888 | 3.7191 | 1.0355 | 3.8512 | 57 |
| 4 | 0.25994 | 0.9656 | 0.2692 | 3.7147 | 1.0356 | 3.847 | 56 |
| 5 | 0.26022 | 0.9656 | 0.26951 | 3.7104 | 1.0357 | 3.8428 | 55 |
| 6 | 0.2605 | 0.9655 | 0.26982 | 3.7062 | 1.0358 | 3.8358 | 54 |
| 7 | 0.26078 | 0.9654 | 0.27013 | 3.7019 | 1.0358 | 3.8346 | 53 |
| 8 | 0.26107 | 0.9653 | 0.27044 | 3.6976 | 1.0359 | 3.8304 | 52 |
| 9 | 0.26135 | 0.9652 | 0.27076 | 3.6933 | 1.036 | 3.8263 | 51 |
| 10 | 0.26163 | 0.9652 | 0.27107 | 3.6891 | 1.0361 | 3.8222 | 50 |
| 11 | 0.26191 | 0.9651 | 0.27138 | 3.6848 | 1.0362 | 3.8181 | 49 |
| 12 | 0.26219 | 0.965 | 0.27169 | 3.6806 | 1.0362 | 3.814 | 48 |
| 13 | 0.26247 | 0.9649 | 0.27201 | 3.6764 | 1.0363 | 3.81 | 47 |
| 14 | 0.26275 | 0.9649 | 0.27232 | 3.6722 | 1.0364 | 3.8059 | 46 |
| 15 | 0.26303 | **0.9648** | 0.27263 | 3.6679 | 1.0365 | 3.8018 | 45 |
| 16 | 0.26331 | 0.9647 | 0.27294 | 3.6637 | 1.0366 | 3.7978 | 44 |
| 17 | 0.26359 | 0.9646 | 0.27326 | 3.6596 | 1.0367 | 3.7937 | 43 |
| 18 | 0.26387 | 0.9646 | 0.27357 | 3.6554 | 1.0367 | 3.7897 | 42 |
| 19 | 0.26415 | 0.9645 | 0.27388 | 3.6512 | 1.0368 | 3.7857 | 41 |
| 20 | 0.26443 | 0.9644 | 0.27419 | 3.647 | 1.0369 | 3.7816 | 40 |
| 21 | 0.26471 | 0.9643 | 0.27451 | 3.6429 | 1.037 | 3.7776 | 39 |
| 22 | 0.26499 | 0.9643 | 0.27482 | 3.6387 | 1.0371 | 3.7736 | 38 |
| 23 | 0.26527 | 0.9642 | 0.27513 | 3.6346 | 1.0371 | 3.7697 | 37 |
| 24 | 0.26556 | 0.9641 | 0.27544 | 3.6305 | 1.0372 | 3.7657 | 36 |
| 25 | 0.26584 | 0.964 | 0.27576 | 3.6263 | 1.0373 | 3.7617 | 35 |
| 26 | 0.26612 | 0.9639 | 0.27607 | 3.6222 | 1.0374 | 3.7577 | 34 |
| 27 | 0.2664 | 0.9639 | 0.27638 | 3.6181 | 1.0375 | 3.7538 | 33 |
| 28 | 0.26668 | 0.9638 | 0.2767 | 3.614 | 1.0376 | 3.7498 | 32 |
| 29 | 0.26696 | 0.9637 | 0.27701 | 3.61 | 1.0376 | 3.7459 | 31 |
| 30 | 0.26724 | 0.9636 | 0.27732 | 3.6059 | 1.0377 | 3.742 | 30 |
| 31 | 0.267 | 0.9636 | 0.27764 | 3.6018 | 1.0378 | 3.738 | 29 |
| 32 | 0.2678 | 0.9635 | 0.27795 | 3.5977 | 1.0379 | 3.7341 | 28 |
| 33 | 0.26808 | 0.9634 | 0.27826 | 3.5937 | 1.038 | 1.038 | 27 |
| 34 | 0.26836 | 0.9633 | 0.27858 | 3.5896 | 1.0381 | 3.7263 | 26 |
| 35 | 0.26864 | 0.9632 | 0.27889 | 3.5856 | 1.0382 | 3.7224 | 25 |
| 36 | 0.26892 | 0.9632 | 0.2792 | 3.5816 | 1.0382 | 3.7186 | 24 |
| 37 | 0.2692 | 0.9631 | 0.27952 | 3.5776 | 1.0383 | 3.7147 | 23 |
| 38 | 0.26948 | 0.963 | 0.27983 | 3.5736 | 1.0384 | 3.7108 | 22 |
| 39 | 0.26976 | 0.9629 | 0.28014 | 3.5696 | 1.0385 | 3.707 | 21 |
| 40 | 0.27004 | 0.9628 | 0.28046 | 3.5656 | 1.0386 | 3.7031 | 20 |
| 41 | 0.27032 | 0.9628 | 0.28077 | 3.5616 | 1.0387 | 3.6993 | 19 |
| 42 | 0.2706 | 0.9627 | 0.28109 | 3.5576 | 1.0387 | 3.6955 | 18 |
| 43 | 0.27088 | 0.9626 | 0.2814 | 3.5536 | 1.0388 | 3.6917 | 17 |
| 44 | 0.27116 | 0.9625 | 0.28171 | 3.5497 | 1.0389 | 3.6878 | 16 |
| 45 | 0.22714 | 0.9625 | 0.28203 | 3.5457 | 1.039 | 3.684 | 15 |
| 46 | 0.27172 | 0.9624 | 0.28234 | 3.5418 | 1.0391 | 3.6802 | 14 |
| 47 | 0.272 | 0.9623 | 0.28266 | 3.5378 | 1.0392 | 3.6765 | 13 |
| 48 | 0.27228 | 0.9622 | 0.28297 | 3.5339 | 1.0393 | 3.6727 | 12 |
| 49 | 0.27256 | 0.9621 | 0.28328 | 3.53 | 1.0393 | 3.6689 | 11 |
| 50 | 0.27284 | 0.9621 | 0.2836 | 3.5261 | 1.0394 | 3.6651 | 10 |
| 51 | 0.27312 | 0.962 | 0.28391 | 3.5222 | 1.0395 | 3.6614 | 9 |
| 52 | 0.2734 | 0.9619 | 0.28423 | 3.5183 | 1.0396 | 3.6576 | 8 |
| 53 | 0.27368 | 0.9618 | 0.28454 | 3.5144 | 1.0397 | 3.6539 | 7 |
| 54 | 0.27396 | 0.9617 | 0.28486 | 3.5105 | 1.0398 | 3.6502 | 6 |
| 55 | 0.27424 | 0.9617 | 0.28517 | 3.5066 | 1.0399 | 3.6464 | 5 |
| 56 | 0.27452 | 0.9616 | 0.28549 | 3.5028 | 1.0399 | 3.6427 | 4 |
| 57 | 0.2748 | 0.9615 | 0.2858 | 3.4989 | 1.04 | 3.639 | 3 |
| 58 | 0.27508 | 0.9614 | 0.28611 | 3.4951 | 1.0401 | 3.6353 | 2 |
| 59 | 0.27536 | 0.9613 | 0.28643 | 3.4912 | 1.0402 | 3.6316 | 1 |
| 60 | 0.27564 | 0.9613 | 0.28674 | 3.4874 | 1.0403 | 3.6279 | 0 |
| M | Cosine | Sine | Cotangent | Tangent | Cosecant | Secant | M |

### 75 Degrees

be displaying 74.739 degrees or 74 degrees and 739 thousandths (74 degrees 45 minutes). This same procedure would follow regardless if you were working with the tangent or sine functions of a given angle. The reverse of these formulas are also true.

The last item to be discussed is the conversion of decimal degrees into minutes. Following are two examples of decimal conversion; both to and from decimal degrees.

**Example #1.** To convert 21', 36" to decimal degrees, read from Tables 7-3 and 7-4; 21 minutes equals 0.3500 and 36 seconds equals 0.0100 decimal degrees. Now add the two together:

$$21' = 0.3500$$
$$36'' = 0.0100$$
$$\overline{21'\ 36'' = 0.3600}$$

**Example #2.** To convert decimal degrees to minutes and seconds, read from Table 7-3, finding the exact or next smallest number; 0.3500

## Table 7-3. Minutes to Decimal Degrees

| Minutes | Degrees | Minutes | Degrees | Minutes | Degrees |
|---------|---------|---------|---------|---------|---------|
| 1 | 0.0167 | 21 | 0.3500 | 41 | 0.6833 |
| 2 | 0.0333 | 22 | 0.3667 | 42 | 0.7000 |
| 3 | 0.0500 | 23 | 0.3833 | 43 | 0.7176 |
| 4 | 0.0667 | 24 | 0.4000 | 44 | 0.7333 |
| 5 | 0.0833 | 25 | 0.4167 | 45 | 0.7500 |
| 6 | 0.1000 | 26 | 0.4333 | 46 | 0.7667 |
| 7 | 0.1167 | 27 | 0.4500 | 47 | 0.7833 |
| 8 | 0.1333 | 28 | 0.4667 | 48 | 0.8000 |
| 9 | 0.1500 | 29 | 0.4833 | 49 | 0.8167 |
| 10 | 0.1667 | 30 | 0.5000 | 50 | 0.8333 |
| 11 | 0.1833 | 31 | 0.5167 | 51 | 0.8500 |
| 12 | 0.2000 | 32 | 0.5333 | 52 | 0.8667 |
| 13 | 0.2167 | 33 | 0.5500 | 53 | 0.8833 |
| 14 | 0.2333 | 34 | 0.5667 | 54 | 0.9000 |
| 15 | 0.2500 | 35 | 0.5833 | 55 | 0.9167 |
| 16 | 0.2667 | 36 | 0.6000 | 56 | 0.9333 |
| 17 | 0.2833 | 37 | 0.6167 | 57 | 0.9500 |
| 18 | 0.3000 | 38 | 0.6333 | 58 | 0.9667 |
| 19 | 0.3167 | 39 | 0.6500 | 59 | 0.9833 |
| 20 | 0.3333 | 40 | 0.6667 | 60 | 1.0000 |

decimal degrees equals 21.0 minutes. Now subtract 0.3500 decimal degrees from the total number of decimal degrees.

$$\begin{array}{r} 0.3600 \\ -0.3500 \\ \hline 0.0100 \end{array}$$

Reading from Table 7-4 we find 0.0100 equals 36 seconds. Our answer is: 0.3600 = 21' 36" or 21 minutes and 36 seconds.

Tables 7-3 and 7-4 are based on one second being equal to 0.00027778 decimal degrees.

## Table 7-4. Seconds to Decimal Degrees

| Seconds | Degrees | Seconds | Degrees | Seconds | Degrees |
|---------|---------|---------|---------|---------|---------|
| 1 | 0.0003 | 21 | 0.0058 | 41 | 0.0115 |
| 2 | 0.0006 | 22 | 0.0061 | 42 | 0.0117 |
| 3 | 0.0008 | 23 | 0.0064 | 43 | 0.0119 |
| 4 | 0.0011 | 24 | 0.0067 | 44 | 0.0122 |
| 5 | 0.0014 | 25 | 0.0069 | 45 | 0.0125 |
| 6 | 0.0017 | 26 | 0.0072 | 46 | 0.0128 |
| 7 | 0.0019 | 27 | 0.0075 | 47 | 0.0131 |
| 8 | 0.0022 | 28 | 0.0078 | 48 | 0.0133 |
| 9 | 0.0025 | 29 | 0.0081 | 49 | 0.0136 |
| 10 | 0.0028 | 30 | 0.0083 | 50 | 0.0139 |
| 11 | 0.0031 | 31 | 0.0086 | 51 | 0.0142 |
| 12 | 0.0033 | 32 | 0.0089 | 52 | 0.0144 |
| 13 | 0.0036 | 33 | 0.0092 | 53 | 0.0147 |
| 14 | 0.0039 | 34 | 0.0094 | 54 | 0.0150 |
| 15 | 0.0042 | 35 | 0.0097 | 55 | 0.0153 |
| 16 | 0.0044 | 36 | 0.0100 | 56 | 0.0156 |
| 17 | 0.0047 | 37 | 0.0103 | 57 | 0.0158 |
| 18 | 0.0050 | 38 | 0.0106 | 58 | 0.0161 |
| 19 | 0.0053 | 39 | 0.0111 | 59 | 0.0164 |
| 20 | 0.0056 | 40 | 0.0113 | 60 | 0.0167 |

# Chapter 8

# BEND FUNCTIONS

Understanding the functions of the bend and how they are applied under actual working conditions is necessary to define measurable dimensions, select tooling, or develop a flat pattern.

Terminology used in this chapter is not meant to be more or less significant than other terms applied to the same function. For example, what this book calls a bend deduction (BD) you may call a "K factor." Please do not put too much weight on terms; instead note the formula at hand.

## BEND CHARTS

No matter how many different bend charts or graphs you may run into, it is rare to find any two that match. For example, the following bend data was discerned from five different charts, with a 1/32 radius punch (Rp.) and a material thickness (Mt.) of 0.060 in. (16 gage).

1/32 Rp. and 0.060 in. Mt.

| | |
|---|---|
| Chart #1 | N\A |
| Chart #2 | 0.063 |
| Chart #3 | 0.083 |
| Chart #4 | 0.097 |
| Chart #5 | 0.102 |

1/16 Rp. and 0.060 in. Mt.

| | |
|---|---|
| Chart #1 | 0.106 |
| Chart #2 | 0.108 |
| Chart #3 | 0.110 |
| Chart #4 | 0.132 |
| Chart #5 | 0.136 |

This is how these various numbers from different charts would adversely affect a standard 1 in. × 1 in. workpiece blank size.

| 1/32 Rp. and 0.060 in. Mt. | | 1/16 Rp. and 0.060 in. Mt. | |
|---|---|---|---|
| Chart #2 | Chart #5 | Chart #1 | Chart #5 |
| 1.000 | 1.000 | 1.000 | 1.000 |
| 1.000 | + 1.000 | + 1.000 | 1.000 |
| 2.000 | 2.000 | 2.000 | 2.000 |
| − 0.063 | − 0.102 | − 0.106 | − 0.136 |
| 1.937 | 1.898 | 1.894 | 1.864 |
| The difference: 0.039 in. | | The difference: 0.030 in. | |

Using the same data, there is an even a greater amount of error over three bends.

| 1/32 Rp. and 0.060 in. Mt. | | 1/16 Rp. and 0.060 in. Mt. | |
|---|---|---|---|
| Chart #2 | Chart #5 | Chart #1 | Chart #5 |
| 1.000 | 1.000 | 1.000 | 1.000 |
| 1.000 | 1.000 | 1.000 | 1.000 |
| 1.000 | 1.000 | 1.000 | 1.000 |
| + 1.000 | + 1.000 | + 1.000 | + 1.000 |
| 4.000 | 4.000 | 4.000 | 4.000 |
| − 0.189 | − 0.306 | − 0.318 | − 0.408 |
| 3.811 | 3.694 | 3.682 | 3.592 |
| The difference: 0.117 in. | | The difference: 0.090 in. | |

Even if the chart that you use for flat pattern layout is reasonably accurate, there is going to be error. One reason: engineers doing the layouts can only be expected to use a chart or median averages for Mt. or Rp. They have no way to know exact material thickness.

Look at the Mt. chart in Table 8-1, using the example of 16-gage (0.059 in.) material. From the mill, the thickness may vary from 0.0548 in. to 0.0648 in. That's a possible 0.010 in. of change from one run of material to the next.

Each variation in material thickness or actual inside bend radius (Ir) will change the mathematical values. But, because operators know exactly what they are working with, they can calculate through these variables and find the exact BD. From there they can adjust for any inherent error even before bending the first setup piece.

## TERMINOLOGY

Before continuing, we must have a common method of labeling things. Table 8-2 contains a list of abbreviations that will be used in the remainder

## Table 8-1. Material Thickness Tolerance Ranges
## for Cold-rolled Steel

| Gage # | Decimal Equivalents | Tolerance Range |
|--------|---------------------|-----------------|
| 7 | 0.1793 | 0.1703 – 0.1883 |
| 8 | 0.1644 | 0.1544 – 0.1734 |
| 9 | 0.1495 | 0.1405 – 0.1585 |
| 10 | 0.1345 | 0.1285 – 0.1405 |
| 11 | 0.1196 | 0.1136 – 0.1256 |
| 12 | 0.1046 | 0.0986 – 0.1106 |
| 13 | 0.0897 | 0.0847 – 0.0947 |
| 14 | 0.0747 | 0.0697 – 0.0797 |
| 15 | 0.0673 | 0.0623 – 0.0723 |
| 16 | 0.0598 | 0.0548 – 0.0648 |
| 17 | 0.0538 | 0.0498 – 0.0548 |
| 18 | 0.0478 | 0.0438 – 0.0518 |
| 19 | 0.0418 | 0.0378 – 0.0458 |
| 20 | 0.0359 | 0.0329 – 0.0389 |

## Table 8-2. Abbreviations

| Label | Name |
|-------|------|
| Mt. | Material thickness |
| Rp. | Radius of the punch |
| Ir | Inside radius of the workpiece |
| $\angle i$ | Degree of angle (included) |
| $\angle$ | Degree of angle (complementary) |
| B$\angle$ | Bend angle (complementary) |
| BD | Bend deduction |
| BA | Bend allowance |
| OSSB | Outside setback |
| ISSB | Inside setback |
| ISTM | Inside through the material |
| ISTR | Inside through the radius |
| OML | Outside mold line |
| IML | Inside mold line |
| D$\angle$ | Die angle |
| Dr | Die radius |
| Dw | Die width |
| $\Delta$ | Springback |
| OSOS | Outside offset |
| MSB | Machine setback |

of this text. Again, do not put too much stress on how terms are named, no matter the terminology the functions are the same. All personnel involved in the bend function should be familiar with bending terminology.

Figures 8-1, 8-2, 8-3, and 8-4 show various bend functions that relate to the terms that follow.

**Apex.** The intersection created by the planes that run parallel to both the inside or outside surfaces of the formed material.

**Bend allowance.** The length of the bend as measured along the neutral axis of the material.

$$BA = ((0.017453 \times Rp.) + ( 0.0078 \times Mt.)) \times B\angle$$

**Bend angle.** The angle created by the inside planes is defined as an included angle and the angle created by the outside planes is the complementary angle.

**Bend deduction.** The difference between twice the outside setback and the bend allowance.

$$BD = 2 \times OSSB - BA$$

**Bend line.** An imaginary line where the punch tip comes into contact with the material surface.

**Inside offset.** Distance between the inside mold lines and the bend line.

$$ISOS = \text{Step \#1)} \; B = (\sqrt{(ISSB^2 + ISSB^2)}) - Rp.$$
$$\text{Step \#2) } ISOS = (\text{sine } (B \angle / 2)) \times B$$

**Inside radius.** The radius formed around the inside of the bend.

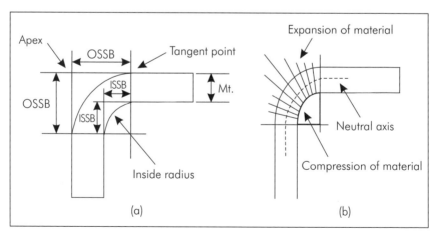

**Figure 8-1.** *The relationships of the tangents, apexes and setbacks through a bend (a). On either side of the neutral axis the material will expand or compress (b).*

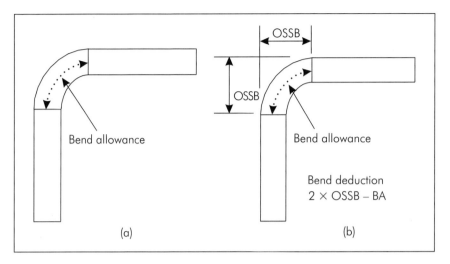

**Figure 8-2.** The bend allowance (a) is the distance around the bend along the neutral axis. View (b) shows how a bend deduction is calculated.

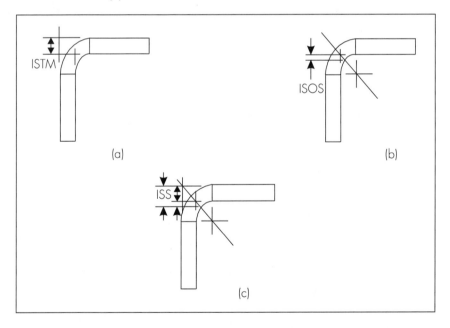

**Figure 8-3.** Inside through the material (ISTM) is the distance between the outside and the inside mold line of the bend (a). The distance between the inside mold line and the bend (b) is called the inside offset (ISOS). The total of ISTM and ISOS (c) is the shift of the bend line in relationship to the outside mold line. This shift is known as the inside shift (ISS).

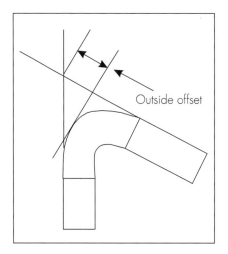

**Figure 8-4.** *The outside offset is the calculated distance between the outside apex and the surface of the material.*

**Inside setback.** Distance between the inside tangent points and apex of the inside mold lines.

ISSB = (Tangent (B∠ / 2)) × Rp.

**Inside shift**. Distance between the outside mold lines and the bend line.

ISS = ISTM + ISOS

**Inside through the material.** The distance between the outside mold line and the inside mold line.

ISTM = (Tangent (B∠ / 2)) × Mt.

**Leg.** Length of the material from the edge to the beginning of the radius.

**Material thickness.** The measurable thickness of the material.

**Mold lines.** Lines that run parallel to any surface (inside or outside) of the workpiece.

**Neutral axis.** A theoretical line within the bend where the material goes through no change during the forming process. No expansion or compression occurs on this axis. Located at forty-four one hundredths (0.44) of the Mt.

Neutral axis = Mt. × 0.44

**Outside radius.** The radius formed around the outside of the bend.

**Outside offset.** The measurement from the surface of the outside radius to the apex of the outside mold lines.

OSOS = ((Rp. + Mt.) / (tangent (B ∠/2)) – (Rp. + Mt.)

**Outside setback.** The distance from the outside mold line to the tangent point.

OSSB = (Tangent (B∠ / 2)) × (Mt. + Rp.)

**Profound radius bends.** A bend in which the bend radius exceeds 20 times the Mt.

Profound radius ≥ (Mt. × 20)

**Radius bend.** Bend in which the punch radius is greater than 63% (sharp) and the radius is no greater than 20 times the Mt.

Radius bend = Rp. ≥ (Mt. × 0.63) but ≤ (Mt. × 20)

**Sharp bends.** A function of the material thickness and not necessarily the radius of the punch tip, a bend radius turns sharp at 63% of the material thickness.

Sharp bend = Mt. × 0.63

**Tangent point.** The point on either side of the bend where the radius meets the flat.

## WORKING WITH SHARP BENDS

It is highly important for operators who work with sharp bends to understand their effects. Not only do we need to understand what is physically happening when the bend is sharp, but we also must know how to incorporate it into our calculations. As previously stated, a sharp bend occurs at 63% of the Mt. and is not necessarily a function of the punch radius. For example:

A material thickness of 0.125 in. (3.175 mm) would turn sharp at 0.078 in. (2 mm):

0.125 × 0.63 = 0.078

This means the minimum possible inside radius is 0.078 in. (2 mm). Regardless of the punch radius, if the bend is less than 0.078 in. (2 mm), it is considered sharp. A punch radius of 0.062 in. (1.575 mm), 0.032 in. (0.813 mm) or 0.015 in. (0.381 mm) would still produce a bend radius of 0.078 in. (2 mm).

Consequently, when calculating bend deductions, 0.078 in. (2 mm) (63%) is substituted for any punch radius less than 63%. Whether or not a bend is sharp must be determined before any decision is made concerning bend deductions, die widths, punch selections, or anything else. If a bend is designed as a sharp bend, and you understand its application, you know that all tooling less than 63% of Mt. becomes valid. Using the example of an 0.078 in. (2 mm) Ir, all punch radii of 0.062 in. (1.575 mm), 0.032 in. (0.813 mm), or 0.015 in. (0.381 mm) are sound, theoretically tripling the amount of available tooling that you have to work with.

### Pinching

The sharper the punch radius becomes, the deeper that a small groove is forced into the material (Figure 8-5). This groove, or pinching, can be both a help and a hindrance in the forming process. Due to changes in material thickness, tensile strength, or grain direction of the material, sharp bends greatly amplify angular variances from piece to piece. The sharper the pinch, the greater the variances.

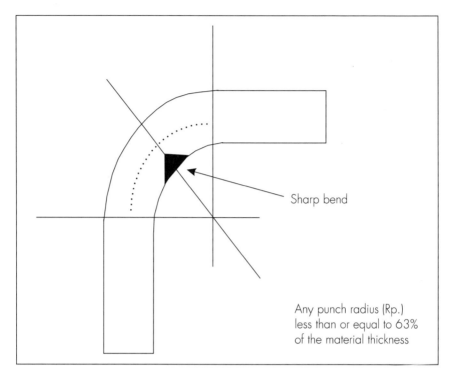

Sharp bend

Any punch radius (Rp.)
less than or equal to 63%
of the material thickness

**Figure 8-5.** *The sharper the punch radius becomes the deeper a small groove is forced into the material.*

The reverse is also true, the closer the punch tip, the less this effect will be encountered. Again, the bend deduction will not change from a sharp bend's 63% Ir. By the same token, you could use that pinch to help bring an angle up to the required degree when circumstances demand an extra small die width to manufacture the workpiece. Whether it becomes a hindrance or assistance is all up to the person doing the forming and his or her understanding of this process.

### Thickness reduction

During the forming process some thinning of the material takes place. In preparing the data for Figure 8-6, we began with the selection of 0.250 in. (6.35 mm) 5052 H32 aluminum. This aluminum is of average common thickness, material type, and tensile strength; plus it is thick enough for the thinning results of forming to be easily seen.

In reading Figure 8-6, notice that "percent of material thickness to inside radius" (Mt./Ir) is shown across the bottom of the chart, and the reverse "percent of inside radius to Mt." (Ir/Mt.) is shown across the

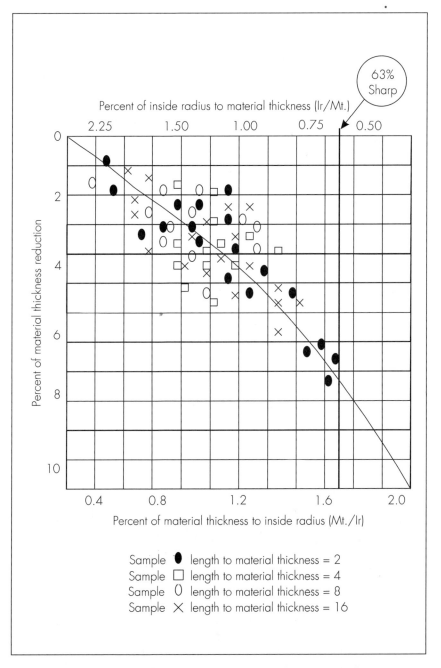

**Figure 8-6.** The percentage of thinning that occurs at the radius of the bend. Note that this thinning ceases at 63% of the material thickness.

top. The top scale starts with a radius relationship nine times that of the Mt. and decreases down to a 0.5 times radius/material relationship.

We begin at the bottom of the scale, reading from right to left, with the "percent of material thickness to inside radius" (Mt./Ir) factor of 2.0. This is twice the value of the Ir. Above it, at the top of the chart, is 50%, or an Ir one half the material thickness. The direct correlation continues throughout the chart.

Reading up the side of this chart is the percentage of material thinning that takes place at a given material/radius relationship. When the relationship is approximately one to one, the material thickness comes in with a reduction of 2%. But, as the radius becomes smaller in relationship to the material thickness, the thinning begins to increase. This thickness reduction ceases to occur when the relationship reaches the 63% sharp bend threshold.

Generally speaking, this material thickness reduction will not affect the forming process or daily calculations. Data in Figure 8-6 is meant to explain where the 63% sharp bend numbers come from and why 63% fits so well into the process. It has been generally accepted that 86% was where the sharp bend occurred but, unlike 63%, no data was available to substantiate these findings. Most of this conflict concerns "air forming." With bottoming or coining, the punch radius is actually stamped into the material.

### Excessive strain

Figure 8-7 shows the relationship between bend length and minimum Ir. Notice that as bend length decreases, a corresponding decrease in inside radius is possible. Exceeding these values, such as with bottoming or coining, will cause excessive circumferential strain, occasionally causing fracturing along the outside radius of the bend. This fracturing varies in different material types, but is greatest in the harder types of materials, T6 aluminum for example. In Figure 8-7 the top line represents a material type of 7075 T6 aluminum and the bottom line is 5052 H32 aluminum. The H32 aluminum is the softer of the two.

Figure 8-8 shows the relationship of bend angle to minimum Ir. The figure shows that the Ir of a workpiece can be made smaller in direct proportion to the bend angle. The Ir of a bend can be made quite small if the corresponding bend angle is slight. The greater the angle, the greater the circumferential strain on the outside of the material. Exceeding the shown values will cause cracking and fracturing on the outside of the workpiece from circumferential strain. Notice the intersecting line running across Figure 8-8; it represents the smallest bend angle capable of producing a consistent circumferential strain.

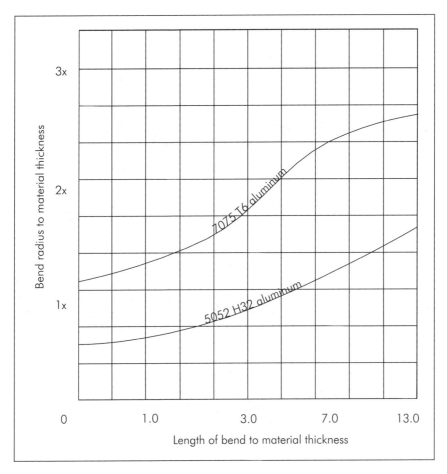

**Figure 8-7.** *The minimum achievable inside radius that occurs as bend length increases.*

Table 8-3 lists one aluminum manufacturer's minimum recommended inside bend radii for several types of aluminum. Table 8-4 shows the same information for several types of stainless steel.

## Material growth, or elongation in the bending process

Many of the different bend functions are, for the most part, self explanatory. Figure 8-2, which featured the bend deduction, showed the amount of change that the material encounters during forming. Some people describe this change as "material growth" and, although the material does not grow, it does change because of plastic deformation. "Growth" describes that change as well as any term. All shape change

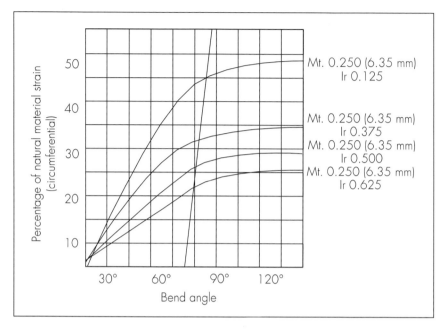

**Figure 8-8.** *Circumferential strain as it relates to bend angle.*

**Table 8-3.**

| Material Type | Minimum Bend Radius to Thickness | | | |
| Aluminum | 0.016 | 0.032 | 0.062 | 0.128 |
| --- | --- | --- | --- | --- |
| 1100 – 0 | 0 | 0 | 0 | 0 |
| 3003 – 0 | 0 | 0 | 0 | 0 |
| 2204 – 0 | 0 | 0 | 0 | 0–1 |
| 5052 – 0 | 0 | 0 | 0 | 0–1 |
| 5052 – H32 | 0 | 0 | 0 | 0–1 |
| 5052 – H34 | 0 | 0 | 0–1 | 1–1.5 |
| 6061 – T4 | 0–1 | 0–1 | 0.5–1.5 | 1–2 |
| 5052 – H36 | 0–1 | 0.5–1.5 | 1–2 | 1–3 |
| 7075 – T6 | 2–4 | 3–5 | 3–5 | 4–6 |

that occurs is accomplished because sufficient stress is induced to exceed the material's yield point, therefore entering the plastic deformation range.

The material cannot be formed to a sharp radius inside and out. The bend deduction is the difference between the outside setback multiplied by two, minus the bend allowance (neutral axis). The excess material is

**Table 8-4.**

| Material Type Stainless Steel | Minimum Bend Radius to Thickness |
|---|---|
| Annealed | 0.5–1 |
| 1/4 hard | 12–5 |
| 1/2 hard | 2.5–4 |
| 3/4 hard | 3–5 |
| full hard | 4–6 |

forced away from the bend, half on either side. This number (the bend deduction), when divided by two, is the amount used to compensate for bending at the press brake, and is called the machine setback.

## WORKING WITH ISTM

Figure 8-3a showed the "inside through the material thickness" (ISTM). It is used to calculate your way through bends where the dimensions are given as one inside and one outside, as in the case of the offset bend in Figure 8-9. If you need to know the flat length from outside to outside, or from inside to outside, it is only simple math.

Outside to outside = side $C$ + ISTM
Inside to outside = flat dimension – ISTM

Use the inside to outside in calculating the flat dimension of an offset bend.

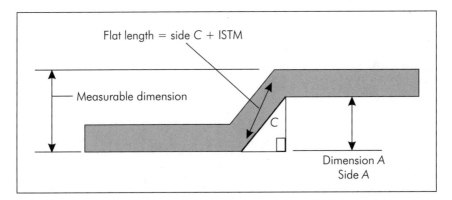

**Figure 8-9.** *Finding the true distance from outside to outside of an offset. This function also can be used to find the length of side A of the offset.*

Figure 8-3, with the inside offset (ISOS) and the inside shift (ISS), described how the bend line shifts during the forming process. When material is formed, the contact point between the punch tip and the material is called the bend line. This line remains constant while every-thing else shifts. Notice the intersecting line running through the cen-ter of the radius and continuing through the center of the bend to the apex. This also is the bend line.

The bend line is in a different location from the inside or outside surfaces of the material.

All three examples in the figure are measurable directly from the outside edge. Take the following example:

1. If the dimension is called from the outside edge to the outside of the bend, it can be measured directly.
2. If the dimension is called to the outside, but you want to measure to the inside mold line, simply subtract the material thickness and measure directly.
3. If the dimension is called to the outside and you want to measure to the bend line, just subtract the inside shift.

Measuring this way is of particular value when measuring bends of less than 90 degrees because of the increased accuracy of the mea-surement.

Last is the outside offset. Moving from or to the outside radius to the apex of the bend, this measurement is used mostly to find dimensions from any given blueprint data.

## WORKING BEND DEDUCTIONS FOR BENDS OVER 90°

Mathematically all of these formulas presented so far are correct; how-ever, there is one important item that we have not covered. When a bend angle exceeds 90°, the true "shifting of material" (bend deduction) be-gins to decrease. It does not mirror the numbers calculated for bends under 90° but it is close (i.e., 135° is real close to 45° in bend deduction). The actual physical bend deduction for bends from 90° to 180° is calcu-lated as:

Machine setback = (bend deduction/2) − outside offset

This number also should be used in the flat pattern development for bends that exceed 90°.

# Chapter 9

# FLAT PATTERN DEVELOPMENT

This chapter focuses on applying the data discussed previously. It features only single axis drawings for the sake of clarity. No holes or notching are included.

Figure 9-1 is a single bend part made of 0.056 in. (1.42 mm) thick material with a bend radius of 0.060 in. (1.52 mm). Together we will find the information necessary to produce a flat length.

Flat blank or shear size is relatively easy to compute. For the following problem, the bend deduction (BD) is 0.099 in. (2.52 mm). To solve the problem, use the dimensions from Figure 9-1 and follow this example:

|  | |
|---|---|
| Flange dimension | = 0.750 in. (19.05 mm) |
| + Overall dimension | = 4.000 in. (101.60 mm) |
| Total dimension | = 4.750 in. (120.65 mm) |

|  | |
|---|---|
| Total dimension | = 4.750 in. (120.65 mm) |
| − Bend deduction | = 0.099 in. (2.52 mm) |
| Flat blank size | = 4.651 in. (118.13 mm) |

The flat blank size equals 4.651 in. (118.13 mm). Repeat this process for both axes. Add up the total outside dimensions and then subtract the appropriate bend deductions, one for each bend.

A word of reminder, bend angles that are identified as included must be converted to complementary angles for all calculations (see Figure 9-2). To convert to the complementary angle, subtract the included angle from 180 degrees. For example:

|  | |
|---|---|
| 180 degrees | = flat |
| − 60 degrees | = included angle |
| 120 degrees | = complementary angle |

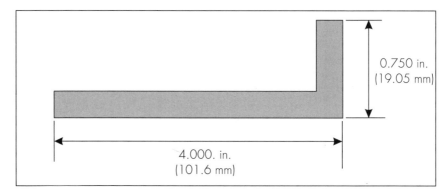

**Figure 9-1.** *A simple single-bend/single-axis part.*

The complementary angle is also the way that most protractors read angles.

There are at least three different ways to find the flat blank. Note how well all the different bend functions from the last chapter work, and how they interrelate. In Figure 9-3 all three major bend functions are represented. They may be used interchangeably to achieve the correct flat blank.

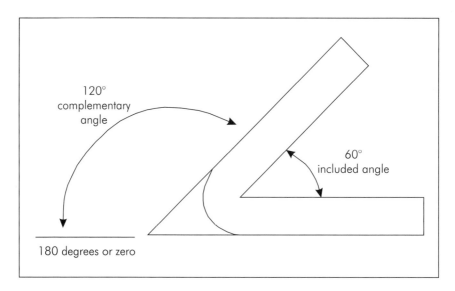

**Figure 9-2.** *Bend angles identified as included must be converted to complementary angles for all calculations.*

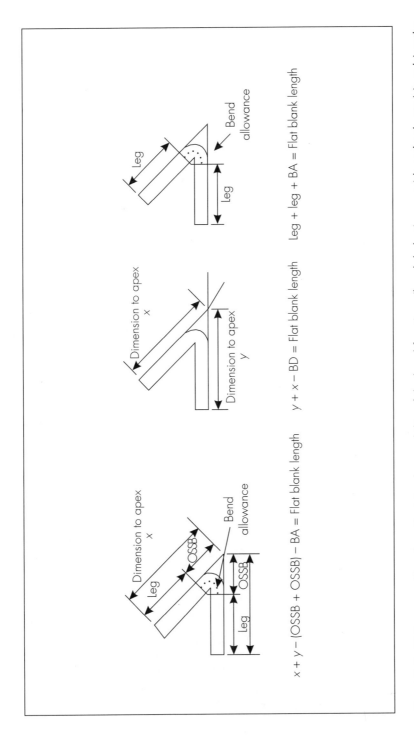

**Figure 9-3.** All three graphics show the interchangeability of the bend functions (bend deduction, outside setback, etc.) in solving the flat blank size of a given workpiece.

# Chapter 10

# READING ENGINEERING DRAWINGS

## ELEMENTS

The basic elements to any engineering drawing are views made up of lines, dimensions, and notes. Lines show the primary shape of the object to be produced. Also included are feature dimensions. Dimensions describe the size and shape of features for an object. They also locate both internal and external features, as well as hole and slot sizes. Notes give manufacturing details that cannot be shown in the form of a drawing. These include (but are not limited to) symbols, abbreviations, types of material, tolerances, and finishes.

### Lines

Engineering drawings include at least one view and generally two or three different orthographic views of a part, which could be of the top or any or all elevations. They also may include pictorial (isometric or oblique) drawings that are added for clarity. The number of views is related to the complexity of the piece to be manufactured. Figure 10-1 describes the basic line types and their uses. Figure 10-2 presents the application of the lines.

There are two different classifications of drawings used in creating engineering drawings—pictorial and orthographic.

#### Pictorial

Pictorials are divided into two subgroups, "oblique drawings" and "isometric drawings," both shown in Figure 10-3. These two subgroups of drawings are normally used for precision sheet metal work when the

*Note: The information in this chapter references ANSI/ASME Y-14.5M 1994.*

| Object line |  ———————— | A solid line | Shows the outline of the piece to be manufactured. |
|---|---|---|---|
| Hidden line |  — — — — — — | A broken line of equal lengths | Shows features or edges not visible in a given view. |
| Center line |  ——— - - ——— | A broken line of alternating lengths | Shows the centers of circles, radius, and symmetrical objects. May be used as an extension line for dimensioning. |
| Extension line | 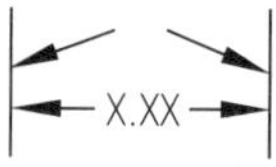 ⊢←→⊣ X.XX | Lines protruding from an object or feature | Lines leading away from a surface or feature that are used for dimensioning a feature size and location. |
| Dimension lines | 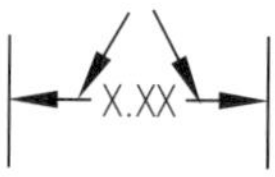 ⊢←↘↙→⊣ X.XX | A solid line with an arrow head on one or both ends | Used to dimension the features of an object. |
| Cutting line |  ↑ ⌐__·_·__⌐ ↑ | Long, thick lines followed by two short lines | Used to define a cutting plane. |
| Section lines | 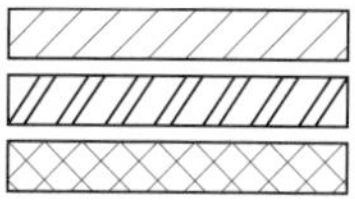 ▨ ▨ ▨ | Different fill patterns | Defines different material types such as iron, steel, aluminum, etc. |
| Long break lines |  —\/—/— | A line with multiple zig zags | Used to show a long break in a large drawing to save space. |
| Short break lines |  ∼∼∼ | An irregular line | Used to show a short break in a drawing to save space. |
| Phantom lines |  ——— - - ——— | Same as a cutting line except that it is thin and not shown on the object | Shows alternate positions of a feature or original material outline. |

**Figure 10-1.** *The different types of lines commonly found on most engineering drawings.*

72

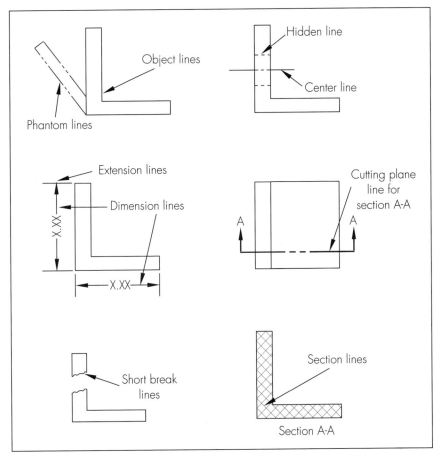

**Figure 10-2.** How each of the different types of lines are applied in the real world .

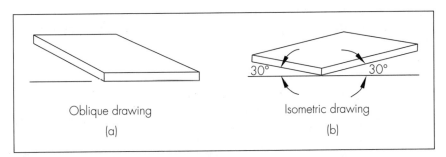

**Figure 10-3.** The pictorial style of drawing is divided into two major types, (a) oblique and (b) isometric.

normal orthographic views do not completely describe the given object. Furthermore, they help the operator have a better concept of what the entire piece looks like in three dimensions.

## Orthographic

Most engineering drawings are done in orthographic. Orthographic drawings are the basic three-view illustration of a three-dimensional object. A discussion of orthographic drawings must begin with an explanation of "third- and first-angle projection." The projection symbol is the shape of a cone containing two views, front and side (Figure 10-4).

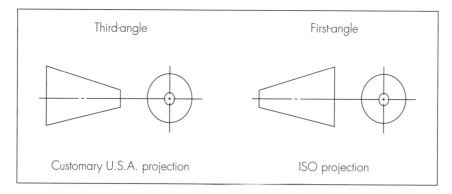

**Figure 10-4.** The customary U.S.A. version of third-angle projection and the ISO (International Organization for Standardization) view of first-angle projection.

Third-angle and first-angle projection represents the way an object is to be rotated from view to view. In the customary U.S.A. version, the cone is rotated so that the small end of the cone points toward the circular view. In the ISO projection, the small end of the cone points away from the circular view. Checking for this symbol and paying close attention to its direction before starting greatly reduces the likelihood of building bad parts.

Orthographic projection drawings have no set limit to the number of views that can be used to describe an object. The normal three views are usually sufficient, but there are times when three views are not enough.

All views in an orthographic drawing hold a certain place on the page in relationship to other views. They have both a vertical and horizontal alignment with adjacent views, as shown in Figure 10-5. Figure 10-6 shows all the possible views for an orthographic drawing. In addition to the standard six views, pictorial drawings may be added for clarity.

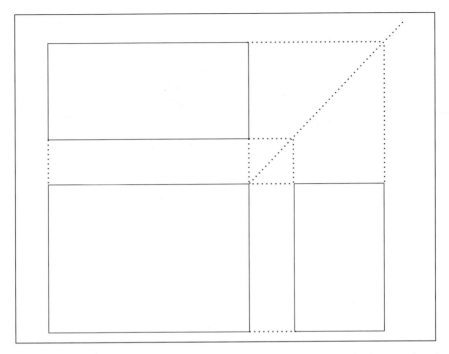

**Figure 10-5.** *All views in an orthographic projection drawing have both vertical and horizontal alignment.*

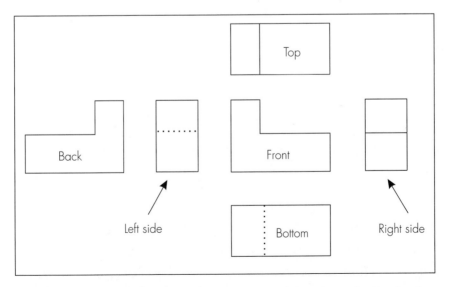

**Figure 10-6.** *All possible standard (six) views in an orthographic projection drawing.*

## Dimensions

To manufacture any piece, the object's size, shape, and features need to be communicated to the machine operator. This is accomplished through the use of both dimension lines with size or location dimensions on the drawings.

A dimension can be called from anywhere on a part, the outside edges, edge to a feature, from inside surfaces, etc. (Figure 10-7). Dimensions also can be called "basic" or "reference."

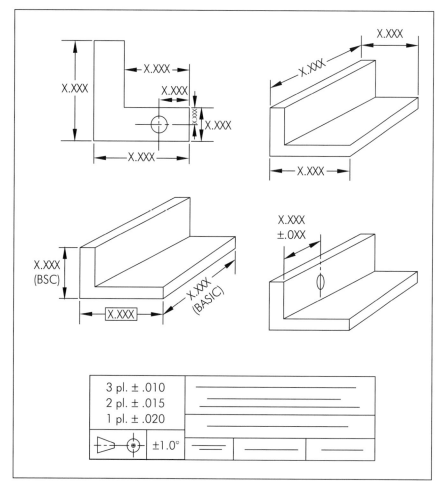

**Figure 10-7.** Location and size dimensions can be called from anywhere on the part to be produced—outside edges, edge to a feature, from inside edges, etc. Examples are shown here by line, with an arrow pointing to the edge and feature in question.

As the name implies, reference dimensions are used for reference only and hold no real weight in the production process. They may provide general information for packaging, shipping, or general inventorying. These dimensions will appear in ( ) such as (2.00) or will appear as "2.00 REF." The current ANSI/ASME standard calls for ( ).

The basic dimension is the exact opposite of a reference dimension in that it is theoretically perfect. Figure 10-7 shows examples of the three ways a basic dimension has been called out on a drawing: BASIC, BSC, or with the dimension contained in a rectangle. The current ANSI/ASME standard calls for the dimension to be placed in a rectangle.

## Tolerances

Tolerances tell the operator how much variation is permissible in the manufacture of a given piece. The general tolerance is usually located in the "tolerance block" in the lower right-hand corner of the drawing or as the feature dimension. This is where the angular tolerance is called out, as well as the third- or first-angle projection symbol.

As a general rule (geometric tolerancing aside), the angular tolerance will be plus or minus one degree (Figure 10-8). This angular variance can be an advantage in forming precision sheet metal, such as in making up material when a part is coming up short on an overall dimension. One degree of bend angle can, and will, drastically alter its dimension. This method of compensation works particularly well when the flange is short in length.

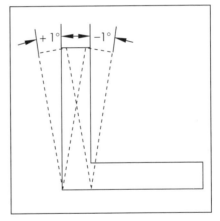

**Figure 10-8.** As a general rule, angular tolerances are plus or minus one degree.

### Terms

Figure 10-9 shows the standard layout of an engineering drawing. Each of the following terms are represented. You will need to refer back to this drawing as necessary.

**Disclaimer.** The disclaimer usually contains the information concerning the ownership of the document along with all of the copyright information.

**General and specific engineering notes.** These commonly cover detailed information that could not be given clearly elsewhere on the drawing. Some examples could be finishes, bend radius, or cosmetic

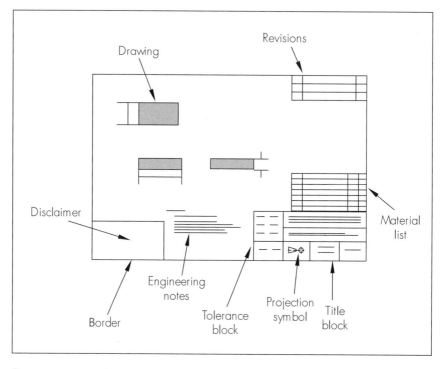

**Figure 10-9.** *Standard drawing layout.*

requirements. These notes can be found anywhere that space or necessity require them to be.

**Tolerance block.** Located in the lower part of the drawing next to the title block, tolerance blocks contain information concerning the permissible variation in the manufacturing process.

**Title block.** The title block accommodates the customer's name and address, part name and number, and engineer's and drafter's signatures. Located in the lower right corner, it will sometimes contain the projection symbol.

**Material list.** Generally found directly above the title block, the material list is the list of all materials required to manufacture the part: hardware, paint, type of metal, etc. In some cases this list can get quite extensive, even requiring a second or third sheet of paper.

**Revisions.** These are changes that have been made to the initial part drawing after the first or subsequent manufacturing runs of that piece or if there are design changes for any reason. Generally located in the upper right corner, it starts with the date and nature of the first revision.

## Geometric dimensioning and tolerancing (GD&T)

Geometric dimensioning and tolerancing is the preferred current standard of part tolerancing. This method of tolerancing encompasses standards that allow greater uniformity of production and assembly. There are many symbols and types of tolerancing included under GD&T. Although many of them do relate to sheet metal production, we are just going to discuss the four types of tolerances that relate most to straight line bending. These are angularity, perpendicularity, parallelism, and position.

Because it is beyond the scope of this chapter to thoroughly describe GD&T, the reader is advised to seek additional training if interpreting drawings is a large component of his or her job.

We begin with the feature control frame and its elements (Figure 10-10). This frame accommodates all control data, including type of control, datum symbol, modifier, tolerance, and reference datums. A datum reference callout symbol establishes a line, surface, or plane and assigns it an identifying letter, such as "A," "B," or "C." These symbols may be attached to the feature control frame. Reference datums are unique to the control frame. They tell you which of the called datum references the controls apply to. The tolerance is the amount of variation allowed as described in geometric terms, with the modifier covering one of three extenuating circumstances as they relate to the control frame (discussed later).

There are over 40 different symbols in the ANSI/ASME Y14.5M 1994 standard. The four that we are going to look at are shown in Figure 10-11. Geometric tolerancing establishes a tolerance zone (Figure 10-12), stated in the feature control frame.

**Perpendicularity.** Perpendicularity, or squareness, describes the zone established by a control frame. It is applied as perpendicularity in

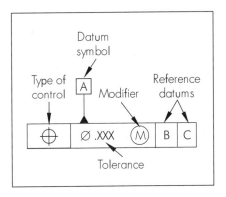

**Figure 10-10.** Feature control frame and its elements.

| Perpendicularity | $\perp$ |
|---|---|
| Angularity | $\angle$ |
| Parallelism | $/\!/$ |
| Position | $\oplus$ |

**Figure 10-11.** Symbols for the four geometric symbols discussed in this chapter.

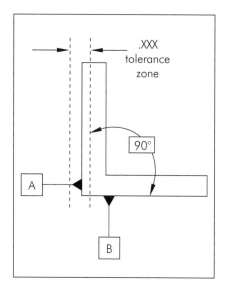

**Figure 10-12.** *Tolerance zone.*

a free-standing state. If any part of the workpiece falls outside this tolerance zone, the piece is out of tolerance and should be set aside for review.

**Parallelism.** When a parallelism control is called, any surface to be controlled must lie between two parallel planes that are set apart an amount equal to the geometric tolerance in the control frame.

**Angularity.** The description of angularity is basically the same as perpendicularly except that it is applied to all other angles, except 90 degrees.

Perpendicularity, parallelism, and angularity are illustrated in Figure 10-13.

These three geometric tolerances are fairly basic and easy to understand. As long as the final free-standing piece lies entirely inside the tolerance zone, the part is good regardless of how much of the tolerance is used. Geometric tolerances generally do not exceed any size tolerance. As a rule, a geometric tolerance is feature specific and the tolerance block contains only general application tolerances. Geometric tolerances cannot violate size or location tolerances.

The last control feature that we are going to look at is position, sometimes called true position. It is arguably the hardest of all controls to understand but one of the most common.

**Position.** There are far too many applications for position tolerance to even begin covering them all here. So we look at the aspects of position that relate to the forming of a sheet metal part, looking first at the basic position feature frame (Figure 10-14a). Its meaning is best illustrated by the visual representation shown in Figure 10-14b. As long as the controlled feature lies within the geometric tolerance zone, it meets the engineering design requirements. If any portion of the feature is located outside of the zone, it does not meet the design requirements (Figure 10-14c).

This type of feature control is one of the most commonly used in the manufacturing industry. It is important to understand how geometric tolerancing is applied to dimensioning. The drawing and measurements in Figure 10-14d describe how geometric tolerances are converted to a linear tolerance that you can directly measure. Figures 10-15a, b, and c look at the features controlled in 10-14d. Under close examination

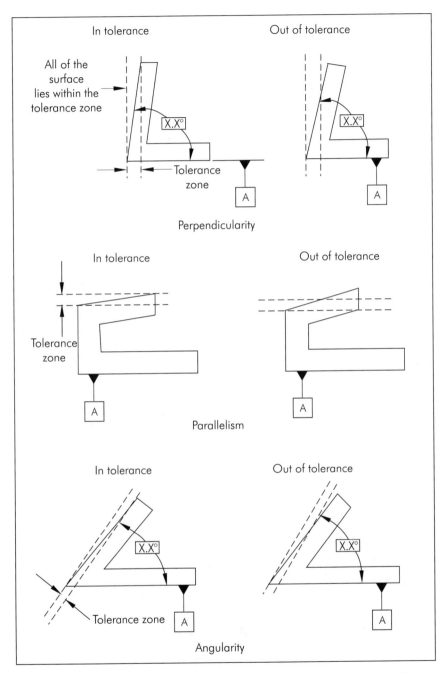

**Figure 10-13.** *Illustrations of perpendicularity, parallelism, and angularity. All geometric tolerance must fall within a specified limit dimension tolerance (size).*

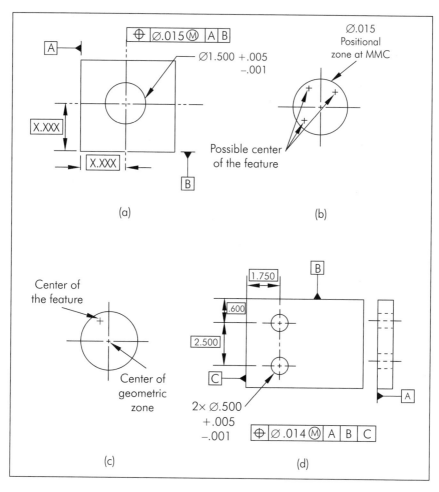

**Figure 10-14.** *Aspects of position relating to the forming of sheet metal. (See fuller explanation on page 80.)*

you will see that this conversion is no more than a simple trigonometry problem.

To do the conversion from geometric tolerance to linear coordinate, use the following examples and formulas:

Total position tolerance × sine 45 degrees = total coordinate tolerance zone

From Figure 10-15a and b: .014 × .7071 = .0099 or .010 (± .005)

Total coordinate tolerance × 1.4142 = position tolerance

From Figure 10-14d: .010 × 1.4142 = .014

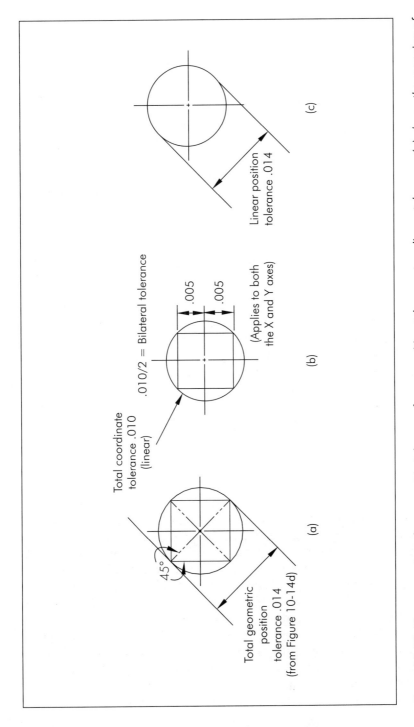

**Figure 10-15.** The conversion of a geometric tolerance from a position tolerance to a linear tolerance; (a) shows the meaning of position tolerance; (b) and (c) the meaning of the tolerance in linear terms.

Total geometric position tolerance .014 (from Figure 10-14d)

(a)

45°

Total coordinate tolerance .010 (linear)

.010/2 = Bilateral tolerance

.005

.005

(Applies to both the X and Y axes)

(b)

Linear position tolerance .014

(c)

In applying a linear tolerance to the feature, the location ranges would produce an acceptable part for the feature located at 1.750 from the datum C (Figure 10-14d).

## Modifiers

There are two different types of modifiers used with geometric tolerancing. "Maximum material condition" (MMC) is represented by an "M" enclosed in a circle. "Least material condition" (LMC) is represented by an "L," and "regardless of feature size" is assumed if ⓂM and ⓁL modifiers are not specified. This type of control is indicated by the letter located inside a circle placed in the feature control frame after the tolerance. In older verions of the standard, the abbreviation Least Material Condition (LMC), Maximum Material Condition (MMC), and Regardless of Feature Size (RFS) may be found. Also, on older versions an "S" is placed within a circle as ⓈS.

When a maximum material condition modifier is applied to the location of a feature, for example a round hole (diameter .250) with a tolerance of + .004 in. (+ 0.102 mm)/− .002 (− 0.051 mm), the applied modifier might be placed at a hole diameter of .248 in. (6.3 mm). In other words, the maximum material condition modifier is applied where the workpiece contains the most physical material for any given feature, or where the part would weigh the most. As the hole approaches least material condition the position tolerance actually increases, or a "bonus" tolerance develops.

LMC is the exact opposite of MMC. The least material condition modifier, when applied to a feature, would define the area of the workpiece with the least amount of material. From our example, the tolerance would be applied as if the hole measured .254 in. (6.45 mm), regardless of its actual measurement.

Both least and most material conditions must be included in the conversion numbers when converting back and forth from geometric to linear tolerancing. For example, with a basic feature hole dimension of .250 in. (6.35 mm), LMC of + .004 in. (0.102 mm), and position tolerance of .015 in. (0.381 mm), we would now have a linear position tolerance of .012 in. (0.305 mm). When the diameter tolerance is divided by two: .004 in. (0.102 mm)/2 = .002 in. (0.051 mm), this amount would then need to be removed from the applied tolerance.

RFS means the specified coordinate tolerance (geometric or linear) will remain in force regardless of whether or not a given feature is .002 in. (0.051 mm) small or .006 in. (0.152 mm) large. Examples of modifiers can be seen in Figure 10-16.

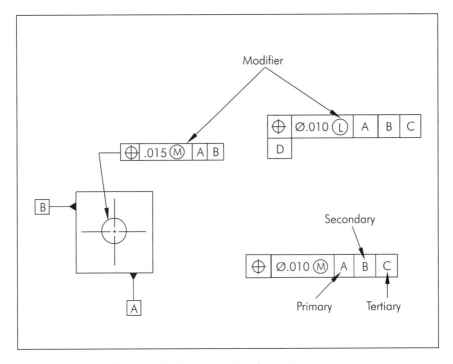

**Figure 10-16.** Modifiers used with geometric tolerancing.

## Basic geometric tolerancing definitions

**Feature.** A general term that applies to any physical portion of the workpiece, a hole, surface, edge, slot, etc.

**Datum feature.** The reference feature used to establish a measurement baseline.

**Datum precedence.** The datum feature order in which the feature's location importance is set.

# Chapter 11

# NOTCHING

Because sheet metal forming does not stop at straightforward bends, notching plays an important role. It relates to the type of tooling used and the order in which the forming is to take place.

## FOUR TYPES

There are four basic types of corner notches, best described in terms of welding penetration (Figure 11-1). The four notches are the 50% weld, 100% weld, closed, and relieved. Each allows for the flange dimension less the bend deduction (BD), plus a percentage of the material thickness that the welding penetration requires.

These notching styles generally are not set by the design engineer, but by the production engineer. The deciding factor is usually the required strength of the corner and the final application of the workpiece. The operator's goal is to produce the correct corner.

### Springback

Figure 11-2 features a 50% weld notch. Notice that the larger dimension on the flat pattern is equal to the outside flange dimension of the workpiece. The lower dimension is equal to the outside dimension less an entire bend deduction. The notch is located halfway between the two lines.

In the fourth type, the relieved notch, the flanges never touch. Of course, if the flange is too large in comparison to the relieve, it can still interfere with the bending process.

All material has a specific amount of springback, which is an important part of the forming order. Springback is the property of metal or plastic to try to return to the flat position. While springback is rarely ever more than three degrees in a small radius bend, it still must be compensated for.

Since springback requires us to bend past the desired bend angle to achieve that angle, the inside bend must be formed last, if possible.

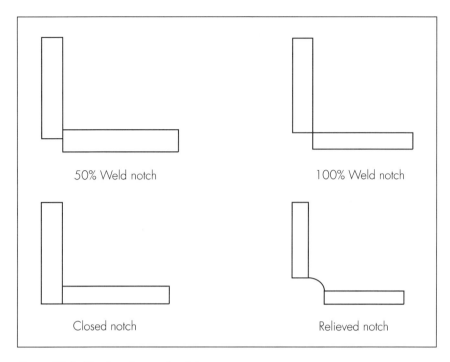

**Figure 11-1.** The four types of notches.

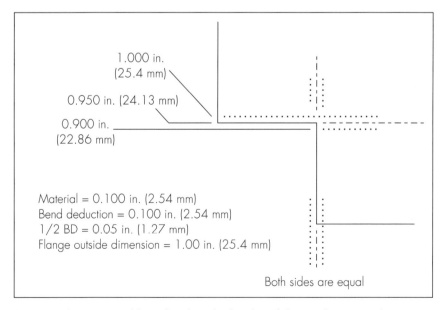

**Figure 11-2.** A 50% weld notch, where both sides of the notch are equal.

If the flange being formed encounters an already formed flange, the interference from that flange keeps the corners from forming up flush. For example, the springback in aluminum is approximately two degrees. If the second bend encounters the first bend at an angle of 90 degrees, the workpiece could not achieve the required 92 degrees. Thus, the corners would remain open at 88 degrees.

Regardless of the angle, under 90° (acute), 90°, or obtuse, the bend that is inside is formed last.

# Chapter 12

# PROGRAM WRITING

## SAVING PROGRAMS

Program writing for press brake controllers involves no more than filling in the data step by step, and saving it to tape or disk. Of course, not all programs need to be saved. In fact, unless the project is either difficult or involves a lot of data, it would probably be best not to save the relevant data.

As long as you do the calculations and make sure that the bend radius is achieved and all angles are correct, you will always make a good part. Not saving every program results in repeated practice that sharpens skills. The possible exception to this rule is if you are doing several pieces of a single job made up of similar materials and common die sets.

### Setup Sheet

For those parts programs that do require saving, both a setup sheet (Figure 12-1) and some form of electronic medium is necessary. A setup sheet normally contains an area for drawing a picture of the part to be formed and for describing the order of forming or gaging. An area also should be included to show the tooling layout along the bed and ram of the press brake.

Along with the drawings, a setup sheet should include:
- tooling locations and the directions in which they are facing;
- types of tooling to be used;
- general press brake settings—lower limits, approach speeds, parameters;
- customer name, part name, and part number;
- where the data can be found—tape, disk, memory, along with location (block numbers);
- a simple sketch of the flat pattern, including the bend sequence; and
- a minimum of step data—exact backgage location, exact bend depth, any step relevant data.

Press Brake Setup Sheet

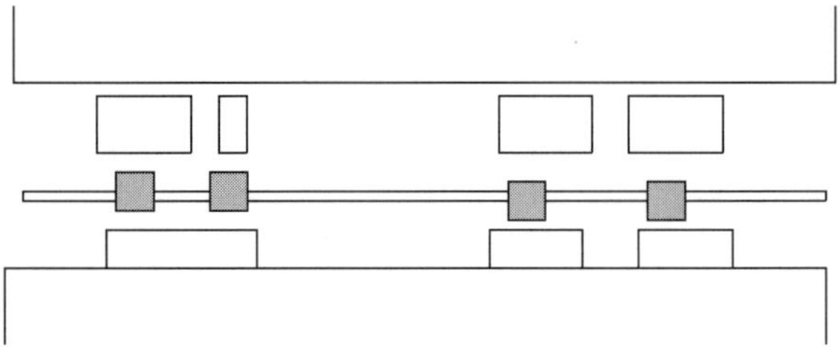

Customer _____ Date _____ Location (tape number) ____

Part number _____ Rev. _____ Block ____

| Station | Backgage | Depth | BD |
|---------|----------|-------|-----|
| 1) | _____ | _____ | _____ |
| 2) | _____ | _____ | _____ |
| 3) | _____ | _____ | _____ |
| 4) | _____ | _____ | _____ |
| 5) | _____ | _____ | _____ |

Die width _____

Punch style _____

Punch radius _____

Die protection _____

Notes:
_____
_____
_____
_____

**Figure 12-1.** Sample of a press brake setup sheet.

Documenting the basic data does more than make it easy to reference the tooling or the flat blank. It also serves as a backup to the tape, disk, or memory. It allows you to quickly rebuild the program if needed.

Each controller has some method of electronically saving the program data. Some store data to cassette tape, others store data to a disk, and some save to a hard drive located at another location (Direct Numeric Control or DNC).

## Formatting

Before any data can be saved to a disk or tape it needs to be formatted. Formatting, in essence, is breaking up the electronic medium into a predetermined number of units or blocks. Tapes and disks usually are not interchangeable between different brands or models of controller. Once a tape or disk is formatted for a particular brand of controller, it is ready for use.

### Blocks

Blocks created during formatting are empty and ready to receive data. When a controller is asked to save data, the reader seeks out the requested block and saves the current data there. The next time you need to rerun the same part, the data will be there to download just by requesting the data in the correct block. The block number and media location should be listed on the setup sheet along with the other information.

When the program is reloaded, some adjustment to the programs is likely needed due to differences in material thickness, tooling, and machines being used. It is good practice to keep a master log, tracking what programs are on which tapes as a quick reference guide.

## Statistical Process Control

Statistical process control (SPC) is a process in which you chart two or more of the dimensions you are measuring. This is to ensure that the customer gets consistent quality parts.

There are many different reasons for using SPC. Numerous types of manufacturing companies have adopted it for use in the shop environment. Often, when producing larger quantities of parts, say 50 or more, SPC is required.

Aside from the Quality Control Department's reasons for demanding the use of SPC, the press brake operator can use the data to great advantage. Used consistently, SPC helps spot trends in the forming. For example, if you are charting every tenth workpiece and notice a dimension gaining or losing material consistently, you can make the necessary adjustments before the workpiece goes out of tolerance.

SPC is not limited to dimensions. It can be applied to angles, radii, and assemblies. In fact, any aspect of manufacturing can be charted.

# Chapter 13

# THE TOOLING

## SPRINGBACK

Springback occurs regardless of bend angle. It results from the compressive plastic, elastic, and tensile plastic properties of a material. As the material is formed, it undergoes compressive and tensile stress (stretch), one on either side of the neutral axis (Figure 13-1). The properties of compressive plastic stress make the material try to stay in the newly formed position. On the other hand, the tensile plastic stress attempts to make the material return to the original position.

On both sides of the neutral axis are narrow bands where no changes in the material occur, so this neutral elastic zone has little or no effect on springback. It is the difference between compressive and tensile plastic stress that develops the springback (Figure 13-2). The amount of springback differs, depending on several factors.

1. The harder a material, the greater the springback.
2. The sharper the punch, the less springback.
3. The larger the die width, the greater the number of degrees of springback (air forming only).
4. The greater the bend angle, the greater the springback. As the angle increases, so does the tensile plastic zone. This increases the springback.

Figure 13-3 shows the relationship of die width to springback. Using the optimum die width yields a springback consistent with the natural springback of the material being formed. Generally speaking, the following springback data is true:

- stainless steel          2 to 3 degrees;
- mild aluminum            1.5 to 2 degrees;
- cold-rolled steel        0.75 to 1.0 degrees;
- hot-rolled steel         0.50 to 1.0 degrees;
- copper and brass         0.00 to 0.5 degrees.

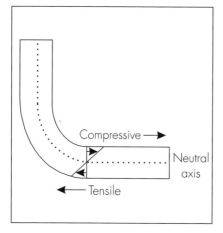

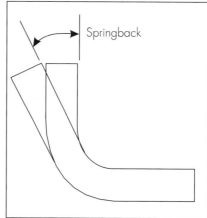

**Figure 13-1.** *As material is formed, it undergoes compressive and tensile stress, one on either side of the neutral axis.*

**Figure 13-2.** *Springback is the difference between compressive and tensile plastic stress.*

## FACTORS AFFECTING SPRINGBACK

The tensile strength of the material, type of tooling, and the type of bending greatly influence the amount of springback. Figure 13-3 shows that natural springback occurs at the point of the optimum die width. Notice how the amount of springback increases in proportion to an increase of punch radius. This increase in springback, also directly proportional to an increase in die width, should be taken into account every time there is a need to vary from the optimum die width.

### Bend Angle

Figure 13-4 demonstrates how bend angle affects the amount of springback across a range of bend radii with the same material thickness. Regardless of material type or strength, bend angle experiences an increase in springback as the bend angle increases.

### Bend radius

It is also true that, as the bend radius increases, the springback increases. This is the most important of all the extenuating circumstances. As the punch radius (Rp.) increases past the point of being profound, a radius/bend relationship where the Rp. is equal to or greater than 20 times the material thickness (Mt.) develops (Figure 13-5). As this occurs, springback starts to increase at a much greater rate than for the standard radius bend. Take the following example:

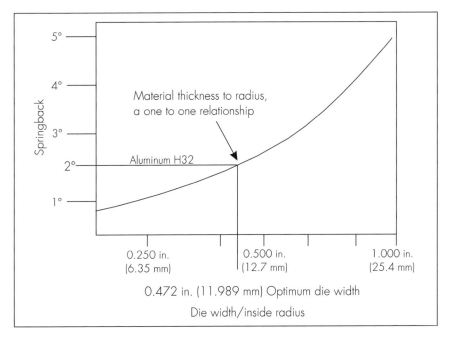

**Figure 13-3.** The relationship of die width to springback.

1. Mild steel with a thickness of 0.031 in. (0.787 mm) and a one to one relationship of radius to material thickness would have 0.5- to 1-degree of springback.
2. In mild steel with a thickness of 0.031 in. (0.787 mm), and a bend radius of 2.375 in. (60.33 mm), the springback increases to 30 degrees.

Why must we be able to predict springback? It allows easier tooling selections, especially in the area of the profound radius bend where springback can increase at least 40 degrees. The calculations, however, work across the board for sharp, radius, and the profound radius bends.

Cold-rolled steel = 0.5 to 1 degree of springback
Mt. = 0.031 in. (0.787 mm)
Rp. = 0.030 in. (0.762 mm)
Actual calculated springback = 0.460 of a degree
Degree of bend angle = 90 degrees

As you can see, 0.460 is not quite 0.5 of a degree, but it's close. You might want to refer back to the decimal degree conversions in Tables 7-3 and 7-4. Coincidentally, this result is also the reason you can bottom or coin with a 90-degree punch and a 90-degree die and still get a 90-degree bend.

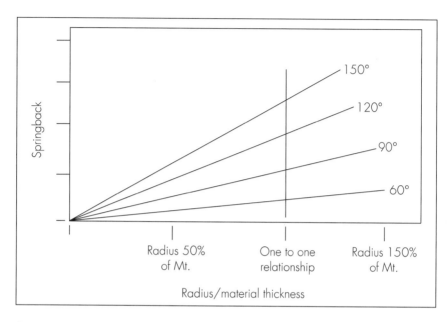

**Figure 13-4.** *This graph displays how dramatically the springback can increase as the relationship of bend radius to material thickness moves toward an increasing radius bend.*

Springback is calculated differently from most formulas. The numbers used in the calculations must first be converted to metric from decimal numbers. This is accomplished using the following formulas:

Decimal number/0.03937 = the metric equivalent (mm)
Metric number × 0.03937 = the decimal equivalent (in.)

Here are some examples:

| Decimal (in.) | Metric (mm) |
|---|---|
| Mt. = 0.039 | Mt. = 1.0 |
| Rp. = 0.787 | Rp. = 20 |
| ∠ = 90 degrees | ∠ = 90 degrees |

The following formulas were used to calculate the data in Table 13-1. The table shows the bend radius to material thickness and the corresponding amount of springback. Using the table, the correct springback for a bend radius of 20 mm (0.787 in.) in a material thickness of 1.0 mm (0.039 in.) would be 9 degrees.

Once the springback calculations are converted from decimal to metric, you are ready to work the formula to predict the springback. The formula is based on mild cold-rolled steel and works regardless of Mt. factors in almost all cases.

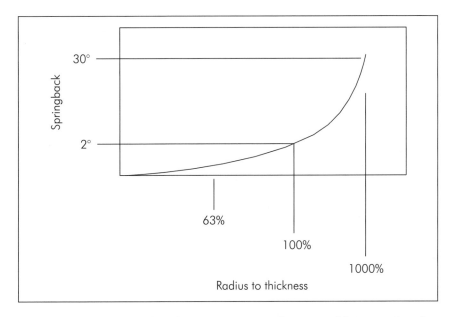

**Figure 13-5.** As the punch radius increases past the point of being profound, a radius/bend develops, where the punch radius is equal to, or greather than, 20 times the material thickness. As this occurs, springback starts to increase at a much greater rate than for the standard radius bend.

**Table 13-1.**

| Metric | | | | | | | | | | | |
|---|---|---|---|---|---|---|---|---|---|---|---|
| Rp.<br>Mt. | 10 | 15 | 20 | 25 | 30 | 35 | 40 | 45 | 50 | 55 | 60 |
| 0.8 | 6 | 9 | 11 | 13 | 15 | 16 | 18 | 20 | 25 | 28 | 30 |
| 1.0 | 5 | 7 | 9 | 11 | 13 | 15 | 16 | 18 | 20 | 22 | 25 |
| 1.2 | 4 | 6 | 8 | 9 | 11 | 13 | 14 | 15 | 16 | 18 | 20 |
| 1.6 | 3.5 | 4.5 | 6 | 7 | 9 | 10 | 11 | 12.5 | 14 | 15 | 15.5 |
| 2.3 | 2.5 | 3.5 | 4.5 | 5.5 | 6.5 | 7 | 8 | 9 | 10 | 11 | 12 |
| 2.6 | 2 | 3 | 4 | 5 | 5.5 | 6.5 | 7.5 | 8 | 9.5 | 10 | 10.5 |
| 3.2 | 2 | 2.5 | 3 | 4 | 4.5 | 5.5 | 6 | 7 | 7.5 | 8 | 9 |
| Springback in degrees | | | | | | | | | | | |

Courtesy: Amada America

The degree of springback is defined as:

$\Delta\angle$ = Rp./(Mt. × 2.1)

For example:

Mt. = 0.8 mm
Rp. = 20 mm
$\angle$ = 90 degrees
Degree of springback  =  20/(0.8 × 2.1)
Degree of springback  =  20/1.68
Degree of springback  =  11.905

This means that there are 11.9 degrees of springback in this material to bend radius relationship. There are still more factors that will have to be taken into consideration when trying to predict springback. Both the tensile strength and the tooling greatly influence the final amount of springback. Aluminum has 1.5 times the springback of cold-rolled steel. Softer metals such as brass or copper have only half as much springback.

Both the table and the formula are based on the air forming of cold-rolled steel. You must compensate for bottom bending, coining, or a urethane backup if they are used.

For other materials, multiply the calculated springback from the formula by the following:

- 2.0 for stainless steel;
- 1.5 for aluminum;
- 1.0 for cold-rolled steel;
- 0.75 for hot-rolled steel;
- 0.667 for a urethane or spring load backup; and
- 0.50 for brass or copper (1/2 hard).

Rework the previous example using aluminum and a urethane backup instead. Starting with a Mt. of 1.0 mm (0.039 in.) and a bend radius of 20 mm (0.787 in.), the formula would read:

Degree of springback $\Delta\angle$ = (Rp./(Mt. × 2.1)) × 1.5 = 14.286 degrees for aluminum

14.286 degrees × 0.667 = 9.529 degrees for aluminum and urethane backup

Degree of springback (aluminum) $\Delta\angle$ = 14 degrees

Degree of springback (aluminum with backup) $\Delta\angle$ = 9.5 degrees

# Chapter 14

# THE PUNCHES

## TYPES OF PUNCHES

There are three types of standard press brake punches—straight, acute, and gooseneck. These are by no means the only kinds of tooling for press brakes, but they are the most prevalent. Figure 14-1 shows these punches.

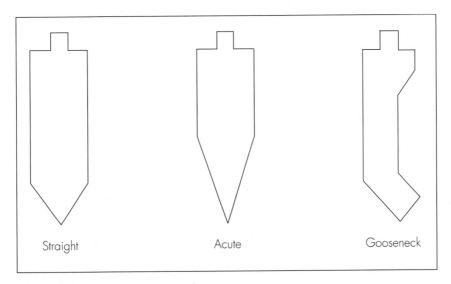

Straight                    Acute                    Gooseneck

*Figure 14-1. Three types of press brake punches.*

### Punch Angle

The first, and arguably the most important factor in the selection process is the punch face angle, which is an included angle. This means that a 90-degree punch will measure with a protractor as 90 degrees, an

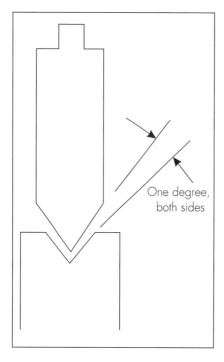

Figure 14-2. *A piece with springback of two degrees would need a punch and die clearance of two degrees—one on each side. Note: there is no clearance required for coining the bend.*

88-degree punch will measure with a protractor at 92 degrees, and a 45-degree punch will measure 135 degrees. Knowing the tool angle, you can account for springback and other factors. To compensate for springback, allow an angular clearance at least equal to the amount of expected springback (air and bottom bending only).

A piece of aluminum with a known springback of two degrees needs a punch and die clearance of two degrees (one degree on each side of the tool set). This type of tooling combination could not coin a bend since no clearance is necessary for coining. Figure 14-2 demonstrates this idea of clearance. The punch and die set allows the workpiece to be brought up to 92 degrees and then released to springback to 90 degrees using air forming. It also allows the workpiece to be brought up to 92 degrees and then forced back to 90 degrees, as with bottom bending.

The included angle of the punch must be equal to or greater than the included die angle. Figure 14-3 is an example of how mismatched tooling could damage the tooling, as well as ruin the workpiece by backbending at the point where the pinch occurs.

## Punch Radius

Now we need to consider the radius of the punch and all its implications to the forming process. A punch radius can be either metric or decimal, depending on the tooling manufacturer. The difference may at first glance seem insignificant, a 1/32 is equal to 0.031 in. and a metric 0.8 mm equals 0.030 in. Using a piece of material measuring 0.036 in. (0.914 mm), in combination with the aforementioned radii, a difference of only 0.001 is found in the calculated bend deduction. But with a punch radius of 1/8 or 0.125 in. and 3.0 mm (0.118 in.), the difference is now 0.003 in. (0.076 mm) per bend.

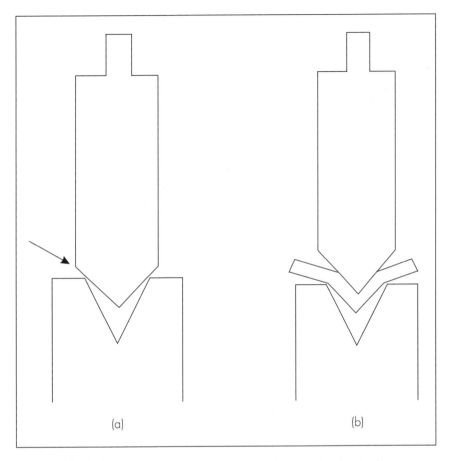

(a)          (b)

**Figure 14-3.** *If the punch has a greater tool angle than the die, tooling contact between them will only be along the top edge of the die (a), which will cause severe backbending of the workpiece (b).*

After several bends, this difference can become substantial. For example, after six bends the error between the flat blank size and the actual required size could be 0.018 in. (0.457 mm). It's true this error is nominal in the general scheme of things, but by using the precision of metrics you deal with fewer errors.

## Sharp Bends

A "sharp" bend relationship can be used to your advantage. Remember, a sharp bend is a function of the material rather than the punch. A punch radius less than 63% of the material thickness is considered sharp by definition. For example, a material thickness of 0.100 in. (2.54 mm) would turn sharp at 0.063 in. (1.60 mm). Any punch radius equal to or less than 0.63 in. (1.60 mm) is also sharp. A punch radius of 0.062 in. (1.57 mm), 0.032 in. (0.81 mm), 0.015 in. (0.38 mm), or dead sharp produces the same bend and bend deduction. This is only true in an air forming application.

If the engineer were to call for a 0.032 in. (0.81 mm) bend radius in 0.100 in. (2.54 mm)-thick material, all the aforementioned punch radii would be valid. The closer the punch tip's radius comes to 63%, the fewer the bend angle problems caused by variances in material thickness or grain direction.

On the other hand, if you need to use an extra small bottom die width, the pinching that occurs may allow you to achieve a bend angle. Increasingly, the smaller the radius becomes in relationship to material thickness, the greater the pinching. Either way, the bend deduction remains the same if calculated at 63%.

## Tonnages

Tonnages can be computed quickly and accurately. Remember, charts tend to be inaccurate. However, by using the following formula, tonnage can be predictable every time. The tonnage per inch can be expressed as:

Tonnage per inch $= ((575 \times \mathrm{Mt.}^2)/\text{die width})/12$

This is the pressure required to bend a 1 in. (25.4 mm)-piece of mild steel in the bottom die width you have selected. Multiply this by the number of inches in a given bend, and that answer is the total tonnage required.

### Applying tonnage

Does the required tonnage exceed the tool's ability to withstand the force? To determine this, first you need the fact sheet for your specific tool to know the tonnage per inch that your tooling can handle. That maximum tooling tonnage per inch, times the number of inches to be formed, equals the total allowable tonnage for the particular tool. The total allowable tonnage minus the total required tonnage gives you the excess tooling capability. *Never exceed the allowable tooling tonnage!*

### Effects of material on tonnage

Because of variances in the tensile strengths of different materials, the formula for pressure is incomplete. As in most cases, the basic formula is grounded in the tensile strength of cold-rolled steel, about 40 on average.

Tensile strength is defined as the ability of a material to bear weight without breaking or being pulled apart under a smooth load or under a sudden impact. Although Table 14-1 is not a complete list, it does include the most common materials used in today's sheet metal shop.

## Table 14-1. Material Types, Tensile Strengths, and Yield Strengths

| Type of Material | Tensile Strength (ksi) | Yield Strength (ksi) | Stock |
|---|---|---|---|
| Steel—plain carbon | | | |
| AISI-SAE 1020 | 27.5 | 15 | Hot rolled |
| AISI-SAE 1020 | 45 | 31 | Hardened |
| AISI-SAE 1035 | 36 | 19.5 | Hot rolled |
| AISI-SAE 1035 | 33.5 | 40 | Cold rolled |
| AISI-SAE 1045 | 41 | 22.5 | Hot rolled |
| AISI-SAE 1045 | 45.5 | 38.5 | Cold drawn |
| AISI-SAE 1120 | 34.5 | 29 | Cold drawn |
| AISI-SAE 4140 | 54 | 47.5 | Full-tempered |
| Beryllium copper 25 | | | |
| ASTM B194 | 35 | 16 | Annealed |
| ASTM B194 | 55 | 52 | Cold rolled |
| Brass | | | |
| Free cutting | 35 | 22 | Cold drawn |
| Stainless steel | | | |
| Type 304 | 42.5 to 92.5 | 17.5 to 80 | Annealed |
| Type 304 | 42.5 to 92.5 | 17.5 to 80 | Cold rolled |
| Type 316 | 45.5 to 75 | 15 to 60 | Annealed |
| Type 431 | 60 to 97.5 | 42.5 to 75 | Annealed |
| Aluminum alloys | | | |
| 3003 | 8 | 3 | Annealed –0 |
| 3003 | 14.5 | 13.5 | H-18 |
| 220 | 24 | 13 | T4 |

*Courtesy: Amada America*

When discussing factors to be used in the pressure formula, a baseline reference is needed. For this we give AISI-1035, the most common type of cold-rolled steel used, a factor value of 1.

The factors or multipliers for various materials are listed below. For any material type not given a factor value, a comparison of tensile strengths allows an educated guess of factor values.

Stainless steel type 304 = 1.4 to 6
Aluminum 6061 T6 = 1.28
Cold-rolled steel = 1.00
Aluminum 5052 H32 = 0.50

Using the factor for stainless steel type 304, the formula would be described as:

Tonnage per inch factor = (((575 × Mt.²)/die width)/12) × the material

Material type = stainless steel type 304

Material thickness = 0.050

Punch radius = 0.030

Die width = 0.236

Bend length = 6.375

Tonnage per inch per inch = (((575 × 0.050²)/0.236)/12) × 1.4 = 0.7106 tons

Tonnage per length = 0.7106 × 6.375 (bend length) = 4.530 tons

Everything involving pressure up to now has been routed around a 90-degree bend in a standard vee die. The maximum required tonnage does not happen all at once, it builds up along a curve (Figure 14-4). Through close observation you will notice that 80% of the total tonnage is developed in the first 20 degrees of bend angle. Even with a small bend angle the pressure on the tooling and equipment can be great.

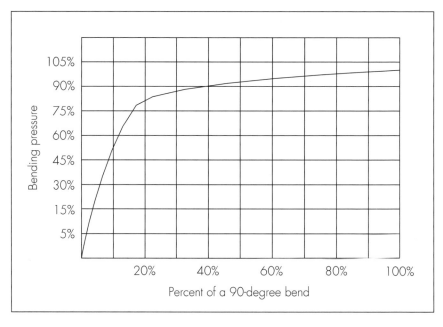

**Figure 14-4.** Maximum pressure (tonnage) builds along a curve, with 80% of the required tonnage being developed in the first 20 degrees of bend.

## Pressure Flow

When mounting the punch into the press brake, special attention must be paid to how the power will flow through the tool. There are two different forms of press brake tooling, European and Standard American (Figure 14-5). Standard American tooling is completely reversible as far as power flow is concerned, but it loses its center in the die. It also loses the relationship from the backgage to the bend line (Figure 14-6).

European style tooling is completely reversible as to centers, but it can be installed wrong. Figure 14-7 shows this type of tooling installed incorrectly. Notice how the pressure flows past the ram and onto the mounting bolts, possibly setting up a dangerous situation.

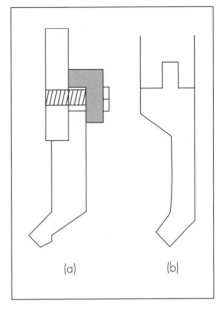

**Figure 14-5.** *Two common forms of press brake tooling, European (a) and Standard American (b).*

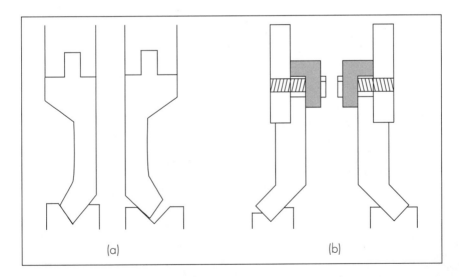

**Figure 14-6.** *Standard American tooling is reversible, but loses its center in the die. It also loses its relationship to the backgage (a). European tooling can be installed incorrectly but keep its center (b).*

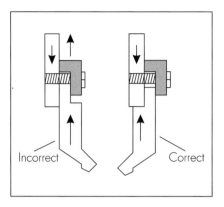

**Figure 14-7.** European style tooling installed incorrrectly and correctly. Note in incorrect installation how the pressure flows past the ram and onto the mounting bolts, setting up a dangerous situation.

# Chapter 15

# THE DIES

## DIE WIDTH SELECTION

There are three basic types of dies in use at this time, standard vee, acute, and square (Figure 15-1). There is very little difference between these three dies except for angle. All the information that follows pertains to the standard vee die. The acute and square dies are covered in a later chapter.

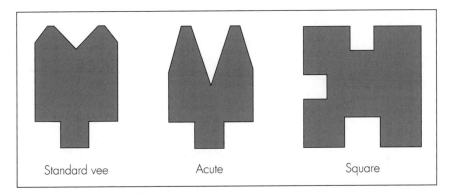

|  |  |  |
| :---: | :---: | :---: |
| Standard vee | Acute | Square |

**Figure 15-1.** *The three types of press brake dies.*

To select a die width in a consistent manner, there has to be a good method of selection.

Most charts and graphs base die width selection on material thickness. Although fine for a one to one relationship between the material thickness and bend radius, it does not take into account the sharp bend or radius bends larger than the material thickness. There are also places where a range of die widths is given for a material thickness. For example, six to eight times the material thickness. Still, this too is only guessing. So where do we start?

We start by figuring the outside radius of the bend. It is very important to take into account the sharp bend in this process. In figuring the outside radius, add the material thickness to the inside radius. But, if the bend is sharp, use numbers generated for the point where the bend turns sharp.

Sharp inside radius = Mt. × 0.63 or 63%

Outside radius = sharp inside radius + Mt.

For example:

Mt. = 0.100 in. (2.54 mm)

Called bend radius = 0.032 in. (0.813 mm)

0.100 in. (2.54 mm) Mt. × 0.63 (sharp) = 0.063 in. (1.60 mm)

Outside radius, *sharp and correct* = 0.100 in. (2.54 mm) + 0.063 in. (1.60 mm) = 0.163 in. (4.14 mm)

Outside radius, *called radius and incorrect* = 0.100 in. (2.54 mm) + 0.032 in. (0.813 mm) = 0.132 in. (3.353 mm)

If the radius of the bend is equal to or greater than 63% of the material thickness, then it is a straightforward addition problem:

Mt. = 0.100 in. (2.54 mm)

Called bend radius = 0.093 in. (2.36 mm)

0.100 in. (2.54 mm) Mt. × 0.63 (sharp) = 0.063 in. (1.60 mm)

Outside radius = 0.100 in. (2.54 mm) + 0.093 in. (2.36 mm) = 0.193 in. (4.90 mm)

From here we would solve for the outside setback (OSSB) due to its relationship to finding the optimum die width. True, the bend angles are not always going to be 90 degrees, but for the sake of die width selection here we set the outside setback as 90 degrees for the calculations.

It is not necessary to work all the formulas from the functions chapter just to find the outside setback. Why? Because at 90 degrees the outside radius is equal to the outside setback. Remember, this is true *only for 90 degrees.* So, for the sake of calculations here, regardless of the bend angle, use the outside radius in place of the outside setback.

Once we have this number, all that is needed to determine the optimum die width are a few simple trigonometry questions. The object of the selection process is to place the tangent points of the bend at exactly 50% of the die face, where the radius begins to pull away from the flat surfaces of the die face (Figure 15-2).

The benefit of selecting a die width based on the outside radius, rather than the material thickness or the inside radius, is that the outside radius is actually in contact with die faces. In this way, no matter how large or small the radius may become, the relationship of the part to the

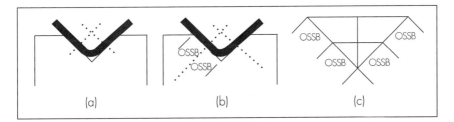

**Figure 15-2.** *In finding the optimum die width, the tangent points of the bend must be placed at exactly 50% of the die face, which is where the radius begins to pull away from the flat surface of the die face (a). In (b), the outside setback has been added. Note: the perfect symmetry of the bend, die face, and outside setback. In (c), the die and bend have been removed, showing the series of right-angle triangles that are produced.*

tooling always remains consistent. Not only is the required radius achieved every time, but so are all the bend functions, thereby increasing the consistency, reliability, and, of course, the accuracy of every bend.

When the die and the bend have been removed, we see the series of right-angle triangles that are produced. It is from these complementary and repeating triangles that we develop our optimum die width.

Figure 15-3a shows only one of the two bottom triangles formed in Figure 15-3b. In this triangle, side $C$ is equal to the outside radius of the bend. Let's take the following example, where side $C$ and the outside radius are equal to 0.150 in. (3.81 mm). Next we need to find the length of either side $B$ or $A$. Because, as stated before, the die width selection assumes a 90-degree die, the triangles then are 45 degrees on a side, making sides $B$ and $A$ mathematical equals.

To prove this equality, let's solve for side $A$, using the trigonometry tables:

Side $A$ = side $C$ times the sine of angle $a$
Side $A$ = 0.150 in. (3.81 mm) × (sine 45°)
Side $A$ = 0.106 in. (2.69 mm)

The first triangle then is illustrated by Figure 15-3c.

Since the optimum die face when divided by two is equal to the outside setback, top or bottom, by simply doubling the outside radius we have side $C$ of the larger triangle. From our example, the die face or double the outside setback would be 0.300 in. (7.62 mm). Just by repeating the same trigonometric process as we did for the smaller triangle, the new dimension of sides $B$ and $A$ is 0.212 in. (5.38 mm) (Figure 15-4). Notice that these sides are also exactly double that of the smaller triangle.

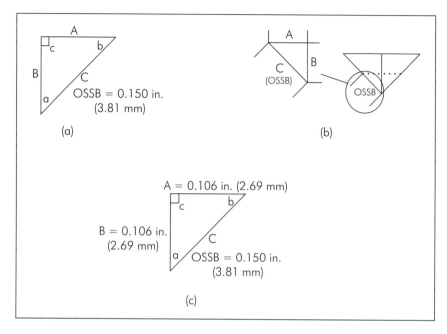

**Figure 15-3.** View (a) shows the outside setback applied to the triangle formed in view (b). View (c) shows the same triangle with the other sides solved.

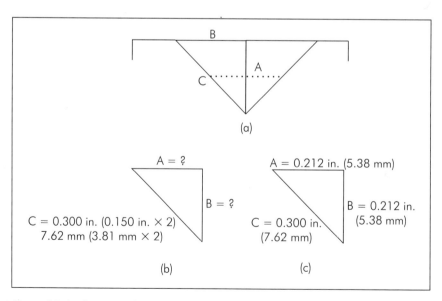

**Figure 15-4.** The same die as used in 15-3, but expanded to a triangle made up of twice the outside setback (a). Views (b), and (c) are of the same triangle solved.

Now put that same triangle back into a drawing of the die (Figure 15-5). Just by multiplying 0.212 in. (5.38 mm) (side *c*) by 2 we have found the optimum die width.

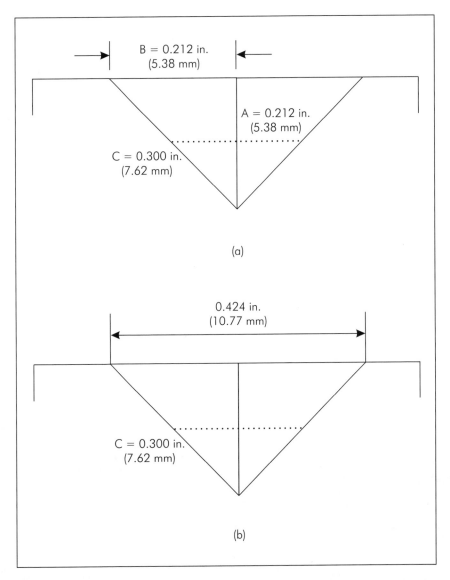

**Figure 15-5.** View (a) is that same triangle used in 15-4 now placed back into a die. View (b) shows the die width being solved for by doubling side B 0.212 in. (5.38 mm) for 0.424 in. (10.77 mm) total.

## Simple Formula

The previous explanation of the relationship between die width, outside bend radius, and outside setback was given for explanation only. It is not necessary to go through this long process just to decide the optimum die width every time you select a tool. There is a simple mathematical formula for figuring out optimum die width:

Optimum die width = 4 × ((outside radius) × (sine 45 degrees))

Figure 15-6 and the following example illustrate how the formula above applies in finding an optimum die width.

Material thickness (Mt.)  = 0.061 in. (1.549 mm)
Punch radius (Rp.)        = 0.030 in. (0.762 mm) (sharp)
Inside radius (Ir)        = 0.038 in. (0.965 mm)
Outside radius            = 0.099 in. (2.514 mm)
Side $C$                  = 0.099 in. (2.514 mm)
Side $A$                  = 0.070 in. (1.778 mm)
$D$                       = side $A$ × 2 = 0.140 in. (3.556 mm)
$E$                       = $B$ × 2 = 0.280 in. (7.112 mm)
Optimum die width         = 0.280 in. (7.112 mm)

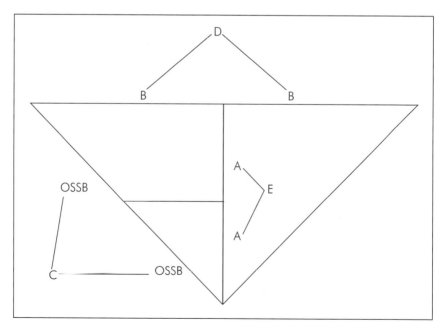

**Figure 15-6.** The development of a die width that has progressed in several parts over the last four figures.

This formula works perfectly where a part has a sharp bend, allowing the sharp bend to compensate for any springback. A radius bend, on the other hand, has to compensate for springback with a slight increase in the die width. In particular, an air forming radius bend needs more of the pre-bend radius that actually precedes the punch tip (Figure 15-7). In fact, you need to draw a little more material into the die opening.

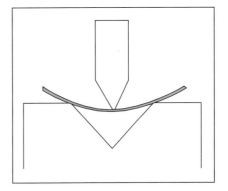

**Figure 15-7.** *Preceding any punch tip is a larger pre-radius bend stretching across the three contact points, the punch tip, and the two upper corners of the die.*

We can compensate for this change in required die width by changing the multiplying factor. For a radius bend in light gage material that is less than 0.125 in. (3.175 mm) thick, we use a factor of 4.85 instead of 4.0. As the material thickness increases, there is a need to increase this factor even more. For material thicknesses of 0.125 in. (3.175 mm) to 0.250 in. (6.35 mm), the factors for both the sharp and the radius bends are increased by a factor of 1. The following factors are for materials less than 0.125-in. (3.175-mm) thick:

- a sharp bend factor is 4.0; and
- a radius bend factor is 4.85.

For materials greater than 0.125-in. (3.175-mm) thick:

- a sharp bend factor is 5.0; and
- a radius bend factor is 5.85.

The information that was just presented relates only to a small radius-to-material thickness relationship. When the radius exceeds 20 times the material thickness, a different set of formulas is required. These are covered in the chapter on profound radius bends.

Is there really a need to be this accurate? Yes, because of the effect the die width has on the inside radius. With air forming, as the die width increases or decreases, there is a corresponding gain or reduction of the inside radius and, therefore, a gain or reduction in bend deduction. Consequently, if you choose a die width of five times the material thickness and someone else chooses a die width of 12 times the material thickness, you would not end up with the same part. This is, of course, not necessarily true of bottoming or coining a bend.

When air forming, there are at least two more important reasons to use a precise method of die width selection. First, as shown in Figure 15-8, the die width increases the amount of ram travel required to effect one degree of change in bend angle. This is assuming that no change in the material thickness has occurred.

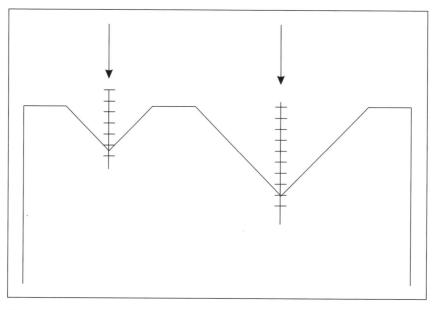

**Figure 15-8.** The larger the die width, the more increments of ram movement required to produce a degree of change in the piece being formed.

Second, the larger this relationship of material thickness to die width, the more shims required to effect a degree of change. Shims are used to correct any error in bend angle.

Of course, you could just shim away at the die set until the error is corrected. But, soon this just compounds any problem with the bend angle, ultimately causing damage to the tooling. With the use of the optimum die width (or as close as possible), more than two shims is usually unnecessary. Normally, if two shims do not solve the problem, there is something else wrong, such as bent or misaligned tooling. Figure 15-9 shows the difference between correct shimming and shimming that can cause excessive crowning.

Crowning occurs when a portion of the tooling is raised, whether or not the raising is accomplished by use of shims. There are several brands of machines that crown by mechanical means. As you can see from Figure 15-9, excessive shimming could cause a die to deform, making subsequent uses of the same tooling more difficult. It also requires at least the same amount of shimming as before to achieve the same angle.

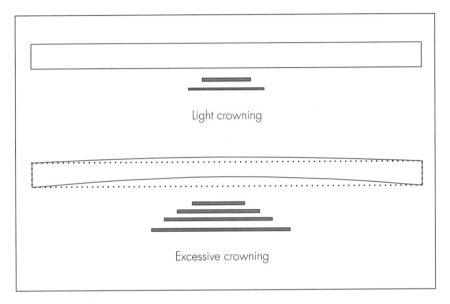

**Figure 15-9.** *Crowning, the addition of shims along the die length to create more pressure at the center, can be overdone. More than two paper shims can cause a permanent deformation of the die.*

## Die Angle

Forming tools come in a standard variety of die angles. Though measured as an included angle, the punch is read as a complementary angle. This style of tools was not necessarily produced to stamp a die angle, such as when coining a bend. Rather, the die angles were changed to help compensate for springback. It is a standard practice that, as the die width increases, the die angle decreases. For die widths of 0.157 in (3.988 mm) to 0.472 in. (11.989 mm) the die angle is 90 degrees; for die widths of from 0.472 in. (11.989 mm) to 0.984 in. (24.994 mm) it is 88 degrees; from 0.984 in. (24.994 mm) to 1.500 in. (38.100 mm) it is 85 degrees; and from 1.500 in. (38.100 mm) and up it is 78 degrees.

## Die Radius

On the top outside edges of the press brake die there is a radius ranging from 0.015 in. (0.381 mm) to about 0.125 in. (3.175 mm). As you might imagine, the sharper this radius, the more likely that die marks are left behind after heading. Die marks, or gouging, are caused by the tendency of the die radius to scrape the material's surface as it is dragged down into the die space.

There is good reason for using both types of edges, sharp or radius. For example, a die with a sharp corner allows you to "catch" the edge of the workpiece when the flange is very small. Whereas, a radius die edge allows the workpiece to slip into the die space, allowing it to slide more freely through the forming process. This also helps maintain a consistent bend angle. There is a point where the die radius gets large enough that die marks will no longer occur. That radius is expressed as:

Mark-free die radius = 1.7 × Mt.

## The 20% Rule

With air forming, the inside radius is never stamped into the material. Rather, the inside radius is determined by the die width. Figure 15-10 illustrates this idea. Take the following example:

Material thickness (Mt.)  = 0.100 in. (2.54 mm)
Punch radius (Rp.)  = 0.032 in. (0.813 mm)
Inside radius (Ir)  = 0.063 in. (1.600 mm) (a sharp bend)

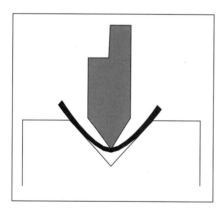

**Figure 15-10.** During the air forming process only, the inside radius of the workpiece is established by the width of the die instead of the punch tip. The inside radius can be expressed as a percentage of that width—20% for harder materials like stainless steel and 15% in milder materials like cold-rolled steel and aluminum.

If the optimum die width were used, the material would float out to its "sharp" radius, 0.063 in. (1.600 mm) in the example. Any other larger die width floats out to a new larger inside radius.

If the material that you were forming was cold-rolled steel, the inside radius would be 15% of the die width.

As yield strength increases, the percentages to multiply by increase. Stainless steel, for example, is 20% of the die width. This works because, when a die width is greater than the optimum for material/radius, the material being formed reaches 90 degrees of bend angle long before the material actually confronts the punch faces. The inside radius can be expressed as:

Inside radius = die width × (0.15 or 0.20)

## Pinch Point

The pinch point is where the punch tip comes into contact with the material, clamping it down against the top of the die. Pinch points are commonly used in conjunction with other controller applications such as in retracting the backgage.

Visualize the pinch point as the die width divided by two (one half of the die width is equal to the depth). Add to that the material thickness and then subtract 0.010 in. (0.254 mm) to ensure a tight grip of the material. The formula for finding the pinch point is:

Pinch point = (die width/2) + Mt. − 0.010

## Hole Distortion

Hole distortion also has a direct relevance to die width selection. As a hole or feature moves closer to the bend line, distortion increases. Any feature that lies inside the area described by the outside setback (OSSB) will distort, with or without a wrap. The least amount of distortion occurs when an optimum die width is used. As the die width increases, the inside radius increases; and as the inside radius increases, the outside setback increases. The greater the outside setback, the greater the distortion area.

## PROFOUND RADIUS BENDS

Profound radius bends are bends in which the inside radius exceeds 20 times the material thickness. The formula can be expressed as:

Profound radius = Ir > (Mt. × 20)

When this relationship is achieved, many changes occur within the forming process, such as the way tooling is selected. However, all bend functions remain the same.

A profound radius bend can be produced by all three types of forming—air, bottom bending, or coining. Large radius bends also can be rolled in a slip roller or formed by bumping up the radius.

### Multi-breakage Phenomenon

Among the important new facets of the profound radius is the "multi-breakage phenomenon," which occurs immediately, separating the material from the leading edge of the punch (Figure 15-11). The result of multi-breakage is that the final inside radius is not only smaller than the punch radius, but it keeps decreasing as the bend angle increases.

While not as pronounced as in acute bends, the smaller inside radius often takes on a distorted polygonal shape rather than a true radius. It becomes more pronounced as material thickness increases. It is also more likely to occur in materials of higher yield strengths (Figure 15-12).

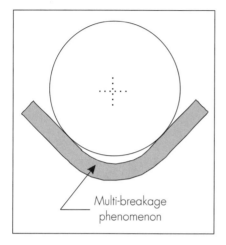

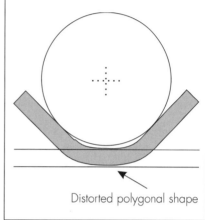

**Figure 15-11.** *Multi-breakage is the radius that precedes all large radius bends. Unless backed up by urethane or spring-loaded dies it will be the final radius upon completion of the bend.*

**Figure 15-12.** *The multi-breakage radius is not a true radius, but tends to be more of a polygonal distortion.*

Table 15-1 shows the multi-breakage radius. This table presents the amount of predictable springback by material thickness and bend radius based on the properties of mild cold-rolled steel. Note: this is a metric table for material and radius stated as degrees.

The multi-breakage phenomenon occurs within every profound radius and at every material thickness. While the table covers only a small range, it can be reduced to a mathematical formula. Not only does the formula cover all ranges of material thickness and bend radius, but it is also much more accurate. The multi-breakage phenomenon can be expressed in the following manner:

Actual inside radius = Rp. – (Rp. × ((Rp. × 0.15 + 0.030) – Mt.))

Obviously this is a more difficult math problem than those presented thus far, so follow along as we go through a sample problem. Remember, always work from the innermost parentheses out.

Table 15-1.

| Metric | | | | | | | | | | | |
|---|---|---|---|---|---|---|---|---|---|---|---|
| Rp. Mt. | 10 | 15 | 20 | 25 | 30 | 35 | 40 | 45 | 50 | 55 | 60 |
| 0.8 | 9.3 | 13.5 | 17.6 | 24.4 | 25.0 | 28.8 | 32.0 | 35.0 | 36.1 | 37.9 | 40.0 |
| 1.0 | 9.4 | 13.8 | 18.0 | 21.9 | 25.7 | 29.2 | 32.9 | 36.0 | 36.9 | 41.6 | 43.3 |
| 1.2 | 9.6 | 14.0 | 18.2 | 22.5 | 26.3 | 29.9 | 33.8 | 37.5 | 41.1 | 42.0 | 46.0 |
| 1.6 | 9.6 | 14.3 | 18.7 | 23.1 | 27.0 | 31.1 | 36.1 | 38.8 | 42.2 | 46.8 | 49.7 |
| 2.3 | 9.7 | 14.4 | 19.0 | 23.5 | 27.9 | 32.3 | 36.4 | 40.5 | 44.4 | 49.3 | 52.0 |
| 2.6 | 9.8 | 14.5 | 19.1 | 23.6 | 28.2 | 32.5 | 36.7 | 41.0 | 44.7 | 48.9 | 53.0 |
| 3.2 | 9.8 | 14.6 | 19.3 | 23.9 | 28.5 | 32.9 | 37.3 | 41.5 | 45.8 | 50.1 | 54.0 |
| Multi-breakage radius | | | | | | | | | | | |

*Courtesy: Amada America*

Material thickness = 0.031 in. (0.787 mm)
Punch radius = 0.393 in. (9.982 mm) (a standard metric radius)
Actual Ir = 0.393 – (0.393 × ((0.393 × 0.15 + 0.030) – 0.031))
Actual Ir = 0.393 – (0.393 × (0.0889 – 0.031))
Actual Ir = 0.393 – (0.393 × 0.0579)
Actual Ir = 0.393 – 0.0227
Actual Ir = 0.3703 in. (9.406 mm)

The actual measurable inside radius (Ir) is equal to 0.3703 in. (9.406 mm) instead of the 0.393 in. (9.982 mm) punch diameter.

There are two ways to prevent the multi-breakage phenomenon from occurring. Both are forms of backing up the bend, with either a spring-loaded steel bar or a urethane pad. Both force the material firmly against the radius of the punch (Figure 15-13), thus eliminating the multi-breakage phenomenon altogether.

## Profound Radius Die Width Selection

Unlike sharp or small radius bends, the method by which we make a die width selection differs greatly for a profound radius bend.

Large width dies, generally over 1.500 in. (38.1 mm), are of the relieved style, but standard vee dies are also readily available. Both types are shown in Figure 15-14. The reason for the relieved die is that the

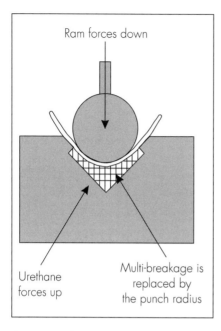

**Figure 15-13.** *A urethane or similar back-up removes all aspects of the multi-break-age phenomenon.*

round shape of the large diameter punch (unless customized) is 90 degrees (Figure 15-15). With the need to compensate for up to 40 degrees of springback in large radius bends, the combination in Figure 15-15 will not work. Because a standard vee die has no relief and the punch angle of a round punch is 90 degrees, the material being formed ends up coined in just two places, as seen in Figure 15-16. To compound this problem, most larger dies have an angle less than 90 degrees, causing the tooling to be angularly mismatched.

With the relieved die, this interface between the punch and die is removed. By being relieved, the punch can penetrate the die space further, bringing the angle to the required degree. The relieved die also allows the changes in die angle to work correctly for the compen-

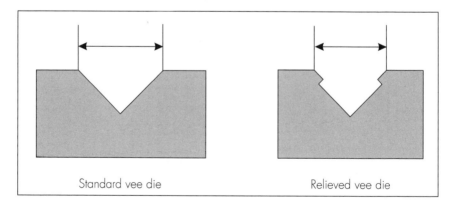

**Figure 15-14.** *A standard American die width needs to be much larger than the relieved style of die. The relieved die allows for a greater amount of springback.*

sation of springback (Figure 15-17). Although the multi-breakage phenomenon appears regardless of tooling type, it is most accurate and predictable when a relieved die is used in the forming process.

There are two different formulas for finding a profound radius bend's die width. One for the standard vee die and one for a relieved die:

profound radius die width (relieved) = 2.2 × (Rp. + Mt.)
profound radius die width (standard vee) = 2.5 × (Rp. + Mt.)

Figure 15-18 represents the relieved die style and how it is measured, an important factor when selecting tooling.

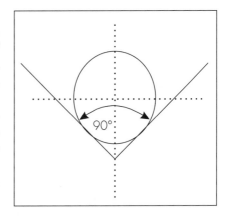

**Figure 15-15.** *Unless customized, all large diameter punches are 90 degrees.*

### Die Angle Selection

To compensate for the large springback factors of profound radius bends, the included angle of the die is changed. This is because die widths would have to become so extreme in a standard vee die as to make it impractical for springback compensation.

After the desired die width is selected and the springback factor is solved, the optimum die angle is easily computed. Take the following example:

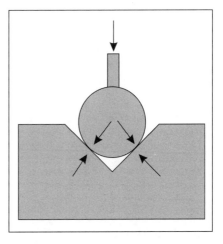

**Figure 15-16.** *Forcing a 90-degree punch into larger dies with angles of 85 degrees or smaller causes the workpiece to be coined only at the point of tool contact.*

Mt. = 1.0 mm (0.039 in.)
Rp. = 20.0 mm (0.787 in.)

As we found in Chapter 13, this combination yields a springback of 13 degrees. Before we proceed, a quick review of some symbols is in order.

$DA$ = Die angle
$B\angle$ = Bend angle (complementary)
$\Delta$  = Springback

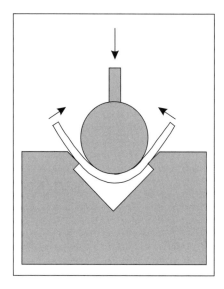

**Figure 15-17.** *The relieved die leaves enough clearance to allow the air forming of large radius bends.*

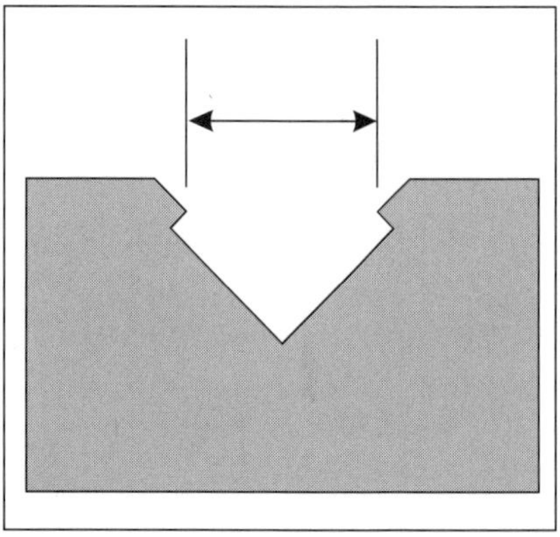

**Figure 15-18.** *Rather than the outside top corners of the die being used to measure die width, the larger relieved dies are measured at the inside top corners.*

The formula for the optimum die angle would read:

Die angle $(DA)$ = B∠ – Δ

Now back to the current example. If we wanted to make a 90-degree bend that requires 13 degrees of springback compensation, the optimum die angle would equal 77 degrees.

B∠ 90 degrees – Δ of 13 degrees = DA of 77 degrees

## Bumped Radius

There is another way that a large radius bend can be formed in the press brake—by bumping the radius up to the required angle and radius. It is of particular value for the production of prototypes or when special tools are unavailable.

There are some terms concerning bump radius that need explanation. First is the "arc length," which is the length as measured along the inside surface of the radius (Figure 15-19). There are many different ways that this length can be calculated, but the easiest is:

Arc length = (B∠/360 ) × 2π × Ir

It also can be expressed as:

Arc length = 6.28 × Ir × (B∠/360 )

Second is the "step bend," which is the number of bends that are used to form the radius and bend angle. The number of times that a bend is formed to achieve the desired workpiece varies greatly depending on the desired results. The more steps used, the smoother the outside radius.

Look closely at Figure 15-20. Assuming that a smooth outside radius is desired, this is what we will use to establish a standard mathematical formula. We begin by dividing the bend angle by two. If the bend is to be 90 degrees, the number of individual bends will equal 45. This makes the angle of each bend about two degrees, regardless of the final bend angle.

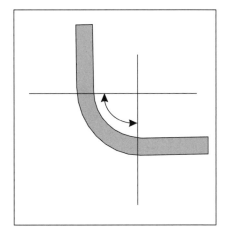

**Figure 15-19.** *The measurement of the "arc length" is along the inside surface of the radius.*

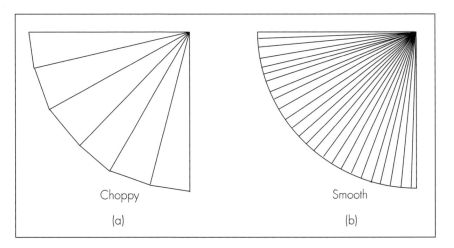

**Figure 15-20.** *The number of times that the material is struck by the punch determines the texture of the radius being formed.*

Third is the "radius pitch," the distance between each individual bend. The radius pitch is found by simply dividing the arc length by the number of steps (bends). Figure 15-21 describes the radius pitch.

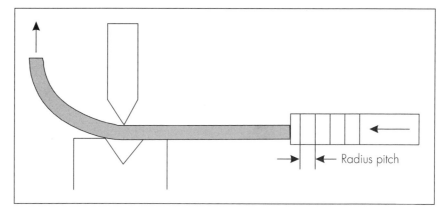

**Figure 15-21.** *The radius pitch is the distance between each strike of the punch.*

### Bumped radius die width selection

For a bumped radius, the die width selection process differs from what we have covered so far. First, using the bumped radius approach does not penetrate the die space to any great depth, only about two degrees per bend. This means that we can use a much smaller die width than normal, since the optimum die width, as normally computed, would be much too large. The optimum die width for a bump radius bend is equal to two times the radius pitch (Figure 15-22a).

This smaller die opening allows the workpiece to lie flat across the top of the die set instead of having one side of the bend lying flat and the other resting on the radius (Figure 15-22b).

However, if Figure 15-22c were used, you would never be able to consistently make backgage contact. Consequently each radius pitch would be in a different location, causing the final radius to vary greatly from bend to bend. Except for some special occasions, the optimum die width for a bump radius bend is expressed as:

Die width = radius pitch (Rp.) × 2

### Punch radius

The required radius of the punch is, to some extent, irrelevant. However, it is best to use a punch radius rather than a sharp bend (less than 63% of the material thickness), and one that is not excessive. The reason for not using a sharp radius punch is simple; a sharp radius punch leaves a more distinct bend line in the workpiece. This, in turn, makes a less smooth outer surface. The reason for not going too large is the small die widths involved.

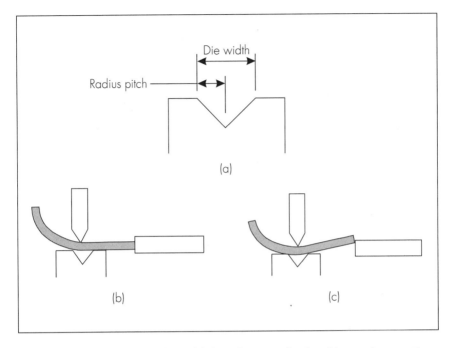

**Figure 15-22.** *The optimum die width for a bump radius bend is equal to two times the radius pitch (a). The smaller die opening allows the workpiece to rest flat across the top of the die set (b). With an overly large die width, one side of the bend could lie on the radius (c) rather than contact the backgage.*

## Depth of penetration

The amount of penetration into the die space has a direct relationship to the die width selected. If you were to select your die width as just described, the depth of penetration would be about two degrees, which is not much deeper than the pinch point, regardless of material thickness. The depth of penetration is therefore stated as:

Depth of penetration = (die width/2 ) + Mt. − 0.020

## Flange

The flange dimension equals the leg (edge to the bend line) of the workpiece added to the length of the arc. This is the starting point, as shown in Figure 15-23. As the workpiece forms out toward you, the end is at the point where the original bend line was established. Note: most controllers require the operator to input one fewer station than the actual number of hits. Figure 15-24 shows how the workpiece is pushed out toward you during the forming process.

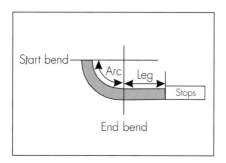

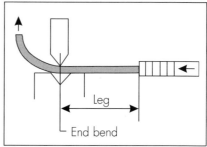

**Figure 15-23.** The flange dimension equals the leg (edge to the bend line) of the workpiece added to the arc length.

**Figure 15-24.** As the workpiece forms out toward the operator, the end is at the point where the original bend was established.

# Chapter 16

# SPECIAL PURPOSE TOOLING

## BOTTOM BENDING

Up to this point we have been concerned with air forming parts of 90 degrees or less. Figure 16-1 shows three examples of tooling angle

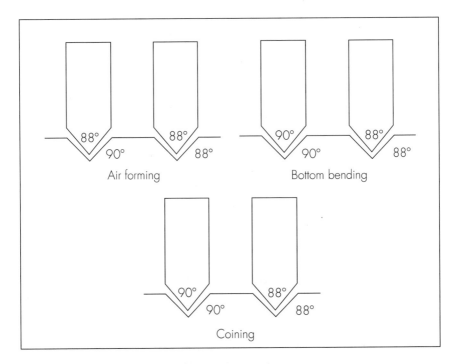

**Figure 16-1.** The different combinations of standard tooling and their relationships to the different methods of forming. Note: depending on the forming process, some tooling combinations may be used by all three forming processes. For example, 88-degree dies and 88-degree punches.

applications for each type of bend. Notice that these tooling combinations have some angles in common. The difference lies in how you use the tooling—for air forming, bottom bending, or coining.

### Air Forming and Bottom Bending Comparison

To begin with, let's compare air forming with bottom bending. In air forming the bend angle and applicable springback are achieved before contact is made between the punch and the die faces. The radius is created by the 20% rule, the inside radius being equal to a percentage of the die width.

On the other hand, using the same tooling combination (88-degree punch and 90-degree die) and applying more pressure creates a bottom bending tool. Increasing the depth of penetration (pressure) brings the material being formed up to the included angle of the punch and then forces it back to the angle of the die. In Figure 16-2, the material is brought past 90 degrees up to 92 degrees (88 degrees included). These two degrees of bend angle are consistent with the springback of softer grades of aluminum.

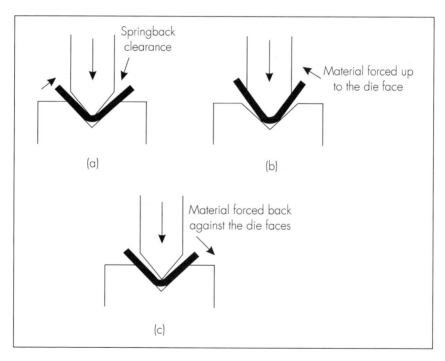

**Figure 16-2.** *In bottom bending the workpiece is brought to the bend angle (a), then past that angle an amount equal to the springback (b), then forced back to the angle of the die (c).*

Bottom bending works well with lighter gage materials and smaller bend radii. It works best in a sharp bend relationship. If bottom bending is done correctly, it requires approximately 50% to 60% more tonnage than air forming. It is expressed as:

Air forming per inch = $((575 \times \text{Mt.}^2)/\text{die width})/12$

Bottom bending tonnage = air forming tonnage $\times 1.55$

## COINING

The principle of coining is similar to bottom bending. However, rather than using an angular clearance, coining uses pressure to compensate for springback in the material. Large amounts of pressure are applied to all mating surfaces, so much that the material yield point is exceeded and the springback ceases to exist. Coining a bend means that the tooling, both punch and die, are of the same angle as the final bend. A 90-degree bend uses a tooling combination of a 90-degree die and a 90-degree punch. Figure 16-3 shows the punch penetrating well into the material thickness, with so much pressure that the material actually flows out away from the bend area.

The tonnage requirements for coining can be from 10 to 100 times the amount of that used for air forming, making coining rarely used in the modern shop. There is much misunderstanding about bottoming and coining. Many people still refer to bottoming as coining, but they are very different bending processes.

Figure 16-3. With no angular clearance, coining uses pressure to compensate for springback. This is done with excessive amounts of tonnage, forcing the punch tip past the neutral axis of the material being formed. So much tonnage is used that damage to the tooling or the workpiece may occur if the procedure is not done correctly.

When using the coining method of forming, it is advisable to use as large a die width as possible to reduce the required tonnage. Remember that large die widths make little difference in the bend deduction because the radius is still being stamped.

Still, it is advisable not to perform this forming process, not only for the operator's safety, but also for the life of the tooling.

# Chapter 17

# ACUTE ANGLE BENDS

Acute angle bends are generally used to achieve bend angles greater than 90 degrees. They also are used as the first step in producing hems or seams. Acute tooling, both the die and the punch, come in two off-the-shelf angles, 30 degrees and 45 degrees of included angle. Figure 17-1 shows an example of an acute die and punch.

Acute tooling is generally used for air forming, but, although not recommend, it also can be used for coining. Bottom bending commonly cannot be accomplished with acute tooling due to limited tool angle selection. Acute tools are not manufactured with built-in tooling angle clearances. This, of course, does not mean that custom tools are unavailable, just uncommon.

Die width selection for the acute bend is chosen in the same way as for standard vee dies. We just ignore the fact that these tools are not 90 degrees and continue the calculations as before. The die radii (the top edges) are still found the same way as for the standard vee die.

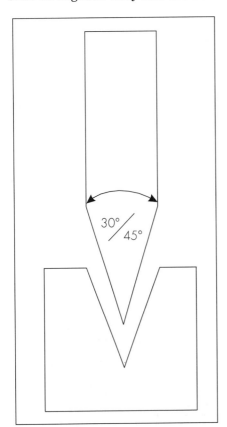

**Figure 17-1.** Acute punch and die sets come in two basic angles, 30 degrees and 45 degrees.

Tonnage also is calculated in the same manner as air forming, because that's what is generally done. Coining tonnage at a normal pressure would likely split the die right down the middle. If you do attempt to coin with an acute tool, use extreme caution.

Bend angles that exceed 90 degrees require a longer minimum flange length so the material forms up to the required angle rather than "snapping" out from under the punch tip.

Figure 17-2 illustrates the differences in minimum flange length; both dies are of the same width, but with different angles. Table 17-1 shows the minimum allowable flange length for acute tooling at a glance.

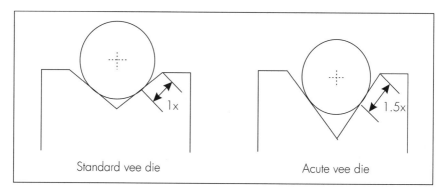

**Figure 17-2.** *The minimum flange length for an acute die needs to be greater than that used with a 90-degree standard vee die to keep the flange from "snapping into the die."*

**Table 17-1. Minimum Flange Lengths between
the 30- and 45-degree Die Sets**

| Material thickness | | 1.6 | 2.0 | 2.3 | 2.6 | 3.0 | 3.5 | 4.0 | 4.5 | 5.0 |
|---|---|---|---|---|---|---|---|---|---|---|
| Minimum flange length (mm) | 30° | 10 | 16 | 24 | 24 | 35 | 35 | — | — | — |
| | 45° | 10 | 10 | 19 | 19 | — | — | 35 | 35 | 41 |

Courtesy: Amada America

## PUNCH RADII

In selecting punch radii, several factors must be taken into consideration. The acute bend actually produces a small flat across the inside of the bend, rather than a true radius. This flat is commonly most pronounced in sharp or small radius bends. Large and profound radii will produce the multi-breakage factor with a totally different effect. The distance across this flat is in direct proportion to the punch radius:

Flat width = the punch radius times two

Punch radius = the flat width divided by two

The rules of sharp, radius, and profound bends still apply even at acute bend angles. For example, the flat of the sharp bend is still solved using the 63% threshold. The use of the flat length, bend radius, and punch radius are shown in Figure 17-3.

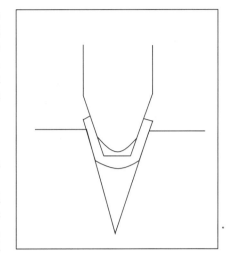

**Figure 17-3.** The inside radius of an acute bend tends to be more of a polygonal shape than a true radius.

Aluminum adds one other aspect, cracking around the outside surface from circumferential strain. This cracking can be kept to a minimum if the flat across the inside is at least two times the material thickness. The minimum allowable inside radius for an acute bend in an aluminum alloy is expressed in the following way:

Minimum acute flat length for aluminum = (Mt. × 2)

Minimum acute punch radius for aluminum = minimum flat length × 2

135

# Chapter 18

# HEMMING AND SEAMING

Hemming and seaming involve basically the same process. Hemming is primarily used for reinforcement, safety, and edge appearance. Seaming is a method of joining two pieces of sheet metal (Figure 18-1). In the hemming process, the bend is started with an acute tool and then flattened in flattening dies (Figure 18-2). The procedure is the same for seaming, except tonnage is increased slightly.

There are two obviously different types of hems, closed and open (Figure 18-3). Selecting which to use is customarily left up to the design

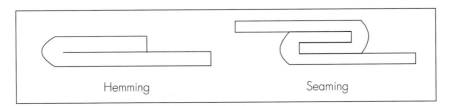

Hemming                              Seaming

*Figure 18-1. Hemming is used mainly for reinforcement, safety, and edge appearance. Seaming joins two pieces of sheet metal.*

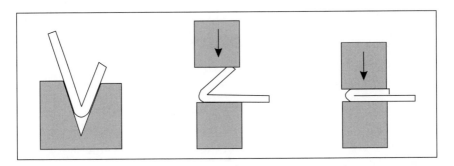

*Figure 18-2. Hemming is started with an acute tool and flattened in flattening dies. Seaming is similar, except the tonnage is increased slightly.*

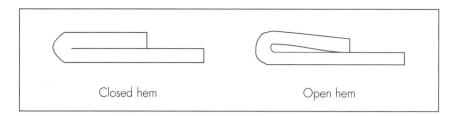

**Figure 18-3.** The two types of hems, closed and open.

engineer. Only the operator will notice the differences in tonnage. Table 18-1 gives the tonnage requirements for both styles of hems using stainless steel and cold-rolled steel. Please note that these particular tonnages reflect tons per meter.

**Table 18-1. Tonnage Requirements for Hems Using Stainless Steel and Cold-rolled Steel**

| Material thickness (mm) | Bending shape | |
| --- | --- | --- |
| | Open hem tonnage | Closed hem tonnage |
| 0.6 | 9 | 23 |
| 0.8 | 12 | 32 |
| 1.0 | 15 | 40 |
| 1.2 | 17 | 50 |
| 1.6 | 24 | 63 |
| 2.0 | 30 | 80 |
| 2.6 | 55 | 90 |
| 3.2 | 70 | 100 |
| 4.5 | 105 | 200 |

Courtesy: Amada America

The formulas for bend deductions, outside setbacks, and bend allowances cease to be of value when the bend angle exceeds 174 degrees. This is because the outside setback approaches infinity. Therefore, the rest of the formulas based on or with the outside setback are no longer of importance.

The blank size is computed through the use of the "hem allowance." In materials with a thickness less than 0.080 in. (2.03 mm), the hem allowance factor is 43% of the material thickness. In Figure 18-4, the piece has a tolerance of plus or minus five thousandths of an inch (0.127 mm) in both directions, which is interpreted in the following manner:

$$\begin{array}{r} 0.059 \text{ in. (1.50 mm) Mt.} \\ \times\ 0.43 \\ \hline 0.025 \text{ in. (0.64 mm) Hem allowance} \end{array}$$

$$\begin{array}{r} 1.000 \text{ in. (25.4 mm) Hem length} \\ -\ 0.025 \text{ in. (0.64 mm) Hem allowance} \\ \hline 0.975 \text{ in. (24.76 mm) Flat blank length} \end{array}$$

In the rare occurrence of an extremely tight tolerance, a pretest of the material should be made to find the absolute value of the hem allowance.

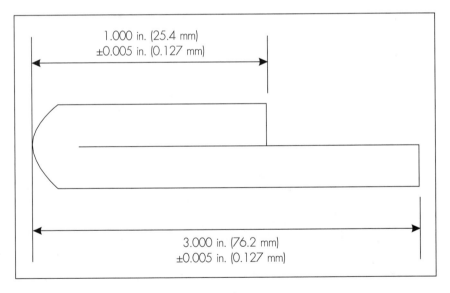

**Figure 18-4.** Tight tolerances applied to a hem.

# Chapter 19

# OFFSET TOOLING

## TWO STYLES

An offset tool is mainly used to set together two bends, bends that would normally be too close for conventional forming methods. With this type of tool there are two different styles, each with a somewhat different purpose. The two different styles are the "upspring" and the "horizontal," shown in Figure 19-1. To determine the depth of the offset required for a given job (Figure 19-2), subtract the material thickness

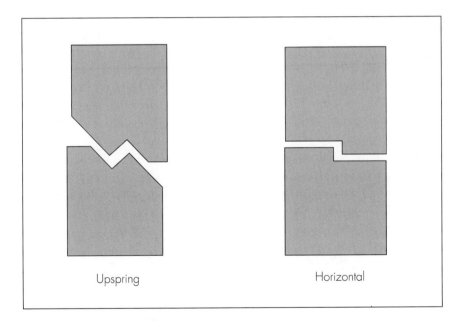

Upspring      Horizontal

**Figure 19-1.** The two types of offset tooling, upspring and horizontal.

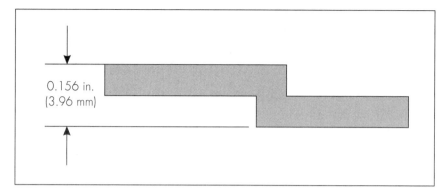

**Figure 19-2.** *To determine the depth of the offset required for a given job, subtract the material thickness from the outside dimension.*

from the outside dimension. The resulting number is the depth of the offset tool that should be used:

0.156 in. (3.96 mm) outside dimension
– 0.059 in. (1.50 mm) material thickness
0.097 in. (2.46 mm) required offset depth

The depth of the offset tool is taken from the measurement between and parallel to the two die faces shown in Figure 19-3.

Determining the punch radius of an offset tool is done in the same manner as a standard punch radius, but it is only found for the upspring tool. The upspring style is a coining tool, designed to stamp the angle at

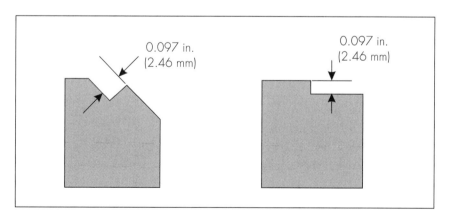

**Figure 19-3.** *The depth of the offset tool is taken from the measurement between and parallel to the two die faces.*

90 degrees, the radius, and the dimension of the offset. Conversely, the horizontal tool, not a coining tool, is used primarily for stepping a material off one material thickness where angle and radius are unimportant and clearance is the main overriding factor (Figure 19-4). The maximum bend angle that can be safely achieved with the horizontal tool is approximately 60 to 70 degrees. Going beyond the maximum causes the tool to shear, rather than bend, the metal.

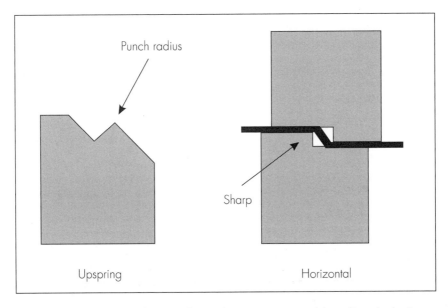

**Figure 19-4.** *Upspring tooling can have almost any reasonable radius; the horizontal offset tooling only comes with a sharp edge. This is because the horizontal style tooling is not meant to bottom or coin. More often it is used to shift the material on thickness at 45 degrees.*

Another important factor to consider is side thrust, which occurs in both types of offset tools, but is most pronounced in the horizontal style. In a standard die set, thrust is applied equally to all surfaces, causing the tooling to sit still during the forming process. But, under some circumstances, the offset tool wants to push out to the side in both directions. If this side thrust gets out of hand, injury to the operator and damage to the tooling or product is likely. Should side thrust become a problem, a thrust plate can be attached to the tooling to keep it from occurring (Figure 19-5).

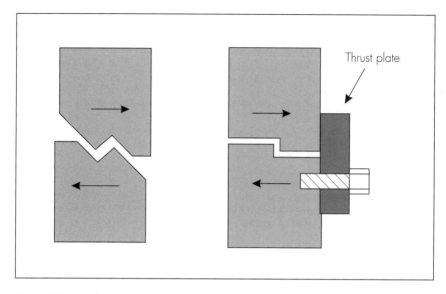

**Figure 19-5.** A thrust plate can be attached to the tooling to keep side thrust from occurring.

Tonnages can vary greatly because offset tools can be used in coining or air forming. Coining produces the best results, but it requires a vast amount of tonnage. Air forming requires much less tonnage, but the final bend takes on more of a "Z" shape than a true 90-degree offset, making calculation of the flat blank, at the very least, difficult without test bending a sample piece first.

## Installation

It is natural to install this type of tooling into the press brake so that the workpiece arcs upward during the forming operation. This is consistent with the course that a workpiece takes when forming in a normal vee die (Figure 19-6a). The correct way to install this type of tooling is for the part to form down as shown in Figure 19-6b. This keeps the backstops out of the die space.

## Variable Offsets (Offset Tooling)

Many times a blueprint calls for a bend angle other than 90 degrees (Figure 19-7). There are two different ways that a bend of this nature can be made. First, with a standard punch and die set, by bending the workpiece to the desired angle and dimension using two separate hits. The second is by using an upspring offset tool.

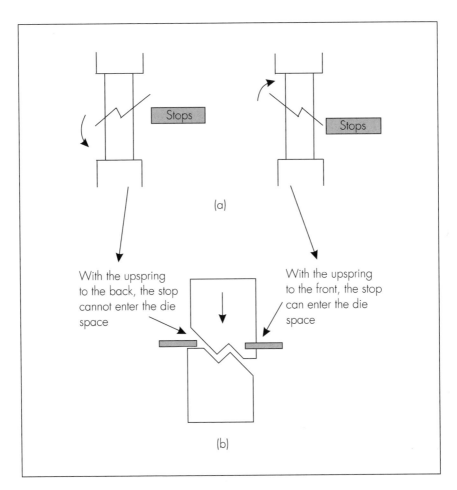

**Figure 19-6.** *View (a) shows the two possible ways an offset tool can be installed. View (b) shows the effect of the installation. Extreme caution should be used to ensure that the stops **do not** enter the die space.*

## The upspring technique

With the upspring technique, a bend angle is accomplished through the use of depth of penetration and the width of the die set. For example, to do a 45-degree offset bend, you need only double the required inside dimension of the bend to find the die width. Multiply the 0.250 in. (6.35 mm) inside dimension by 2 to get 0.500 in. (12.7 mm). Five hundred thousandths (12.7 mm) would then be the die width of the offset. To achieve the angle we need to penetrate the die space by only 50%.

In Figure 19-8 you see this principle at work, regardless of the angle or dimension. All of these pieces could be easily produced in the same 0.500 in. (12.7 mm) offset.

This process can be expressed in mathematical formulas, which work well with any angle less than 90 degrees. The following is a list of the variables and formulas.

The variables:

$A$ = Required inside dimension
$A \angle$ = Side $A$ of offset triangle
$B$ = Actual measured tool dimension
Dp = Developed penetration
Od = Optimum die width

The formulas:

Optimum die width (Od) = $A \angle /0.7071$
Developed penetration (Dp) = $((B \times 0.7071) + 0.046) - (A/2)$
Actual machine input depth = Dp

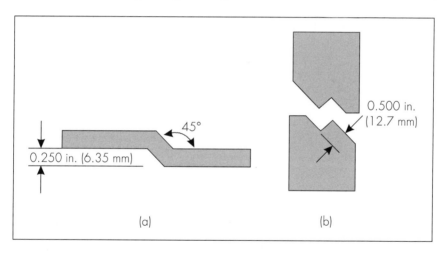

*Figure 19-7.* To achieve a 0.250 in. (6.35 mm) offset (a) at 45 degrees, we double the 0.250 dimension to 0.500 in. (12.7 mm). The 0.500 in. dimension is the offset tool dimension (b). When the workpiece is formed, the die space will be penetrated to 50%—one half of the die angle equals 45 degrees and one half the dimension equals 0.250 in.

These formulas are another example of the applications of right-angle trigonometry in precision sheet metal forming. Figure 19-9 is always true regardless of the angle or dimension. (Excluding material and part length variables, the input depth will be close.)

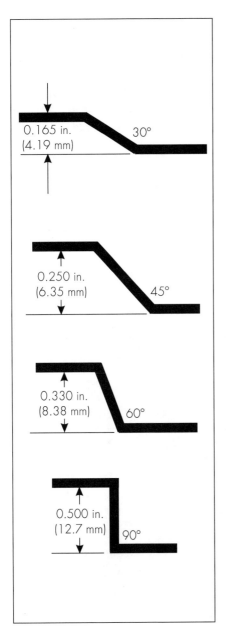

**Figure 19-8.** *The views shown here could be accomplished with the same tooling set. It is just a matter of punch penetration into the die space.*

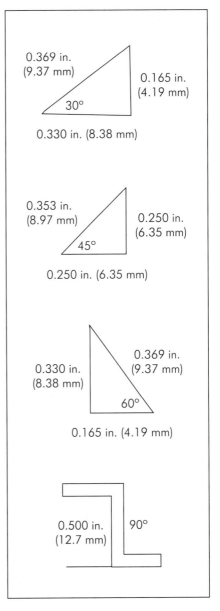

**Figure 19-9.** *These views are the same offsets shown in Figure 19-8, but described as triangles. Notice how the dimensions shift around the triangle as the depth continues to increase.*

If a 30-degree offset with a dimension of 0.165 in. (4.19 mm) on the *A* side of the triangle is achieved, the *C* and *B* sides are also achieved. Follow the progression of the angle and the dimension as it reaches 0.500 in. (12.7 mm) at 90 degrees.

As you can see in Figure 19-10, the material is being pulled down into the die space. Side *C* increases in direct proportion to the depth of penetration, side *A*. The bend angle also changes in direct relationship to the change in penetration.

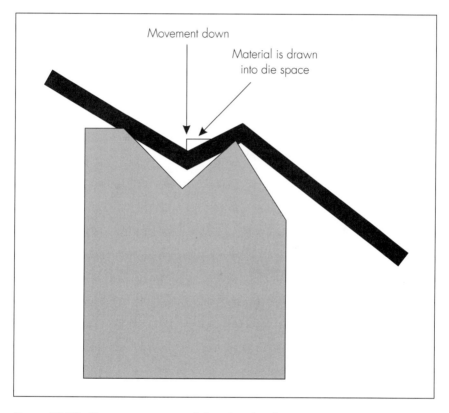

**Figure 19-10.** *Here we see one of the triangles from Figure 19-9 applied to a workpiece and die set. Notice how the material is drawn into the die space. As the depth of penetration increases, side C of the triangle increases.*

If the calculated die width is unavailable, you may have to estimate a little on either the bend angle or the dimension to produce a good part. That is the reason for the "actual measured tool dimension (*B*)" in our formulas. If possible, it is better to cheat the bend angle instead of the dimension because the dimension is much easier to measure. The angle can easily be checked by ensuring that the dimensions are correct; the rest is right-angle trigonometry.

## Standard punch and die

The second way a variable angle offset bend can be produced is by using a standard punch and die set. It is accomplished by stepping the bend out toward you, starting with the inside bend first, as shown in Figure 19-11. This two-step process for setting up this type of bend is easy. First, you find the inside bend line as shown in Figure 19-12.

Step #1 = side $C$ + flange dimension – bend deduction

Second, you find the bend line of the second bend.

Step #2 = flange dimension – bend deduction/2

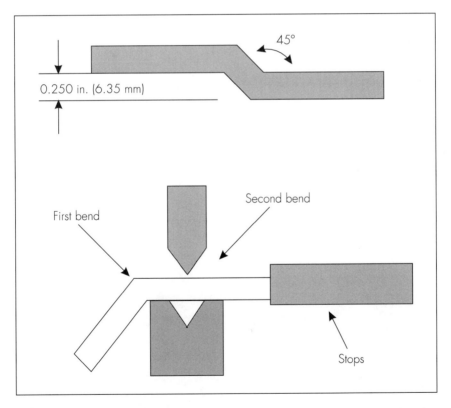

**Figure 19-11.** An offset bend can be done in a two-step process, stepping the workpiece out toward you.

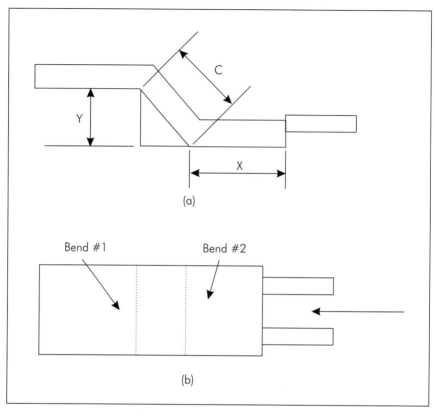

**Figure 19-12.** Method by which the bend lines are located for a two-step off-set bend.

# Chapter 20

# URETHANE TOOLING

The use of urethane tooling at the press brake is relatively new (circa 1980), and many press brake operators do not yet understand, or even know about it.

Urethane tooling is a variation of the traditional press brake steel punch and die sets, except the die is replaced by a urethane elastomer (Figure 20-1). It can offer some advantages and outperforms standard tooling in some applications.

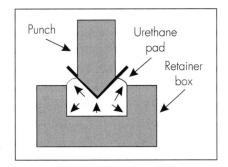

**Figure 20-1.** Sectional view of the urethane forming process.

## ADVANTAGES AND DISADVANTAGES

Compared to other elastic materials, such as rubber or plastic, urethane has a higher resiliency to impact and greater tensile strength. It is resistant to both oils and acid, making it well suited for use in forming sheet metal.

In the urethane family, polyether urethane is the most common type used in press brake tooling.

Urethane tooling makes setups and programming easier, and increases the range of forming to such applications as complex curves.

**Advantages of urethane tooling.**

1. Setup time is reduced because die and punch matching and alignment is not necessary.
2. Allows for good dimensional stability; workpieces encounter less springback (about two thirds of normal).
3. Totally eliminates the multi-breakage phenomenon.

4. Acts as a fluid, absorbing all side thrust.
5. Die and punch changes become less common with factors like die and punch angle, material thickness, and radius changes.
6. No marring of the workpiece.
7. Bend angles up to 180 degrees.
8. Urethane makes an excellent die for use with a 30-degree/60-degree punch. It overcomes the side thrust associated with 30-degree/60-degree tooling.
9. It is excellent for special purpose forming, for example, stamping, swaging, and embossing.

**Disadvantages of urethane tooling**.

1. Short life span compared to steel.
2. Tonnage requirements of urethane tooling are far greater than those of standard steel tooling.
3. Not suitable for use on small dimension flanges.
4. Urethane works well with only light gage materials. Thicker materials have too much tonnage for practical use.
5. High cost of the retainer box.
6. Urethane tooling can become impregnated with small pieces of metal that can mar the workpiece.

## TERMS

There are several terms associated specifically with urethane tooling:

**Die pad.** A square or rectangular pad of urethane.

**Retainer box.** The metal box used to contain the die pad.

**Deflection bars.** Round bars placed inside the retainer box to help produce a more complete and consistent bend.

**Overbending**. Bending past the required bend angle by as much as 40 degrees.

**Unbalanced tooling.** Punches with angles of 30/60 degrees rather than 45/45 degrees.

## CHARACTERISTICS

Urethane tooling is divided into two groups, deflecting and nondeflecting. The deflecting group is divided further into four subgroups, each with its own amount of deflection. Deflection is measured on a durometer and is recorded on either the A or D scales.

(0) — soft, 35% deflection, 80A duro.
(1) — medium, 25% deflection, 90A duro.

(2) — hard, 15% deflection, 95A duro.

(3) — very hard, 5% deflection, 75D duro.

Different grades of urethane are color coded and can be quickly and easily identified.

Hardness grade (0) is red. Its uses include: vee bends, unbalanced vee bends, U-bends, and special application tools. Grade (1) is blue. Its uses include: vee bends, unbalanced vee bends, U-bends, unbalanced U-bends, and special application tooling. Hardness grade (2) is yellow and primarily used for vee and U-bends. Grade (3) is white and used mainly for special applications.

## Urethane Pads

The most common reason for urethane pad failure is hysteresis, the buildup of internal heat within the pad itself. The correct selection of grade and deflection is necessary for the life of the pad. Urethane is not inexpensive.

The most common type of urethane tooling is usually a square or rectangular pad contained inside the retainer box. As pressure is applied to the pad the urethane begins to act as a liquid (deflection). This in turn produces equal pressure on all the surfaces in contact with the pad, both the inside faces of the retainer box as well as around the entire working surface of the material formed.

In the standard vee die, all the force is applied only along straight lines where there is an interaction between the die faces, the material, and the punch. However, in the case of urethane tooling, as the punch begins to penetrate the urethane pad, the applied force is transferred to the pad, which then transfers the pressure equally to all points shown in Figure 20-2.

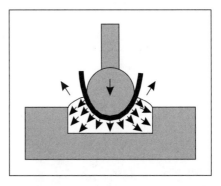

The retainer box prevents deflection on five sides of the urethane pad, causing the pad to deflect upward and around the punch radius or tip. It does this because it has nowhere else to go (Figure 20-3). This upward movement acts to force the material to wrap around the radius allowing

**Figure 20-2.** In the case of urethane tooling, as the punch begins to penetrate the urethane pad, the applied force is transferred to the pad, which then transfers pressure equally to all points shown. In the standard vee die, force is applied only along straight lines where there is interaction between the die face, material, and punch.

153

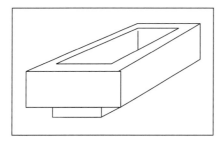

**Figure 20-3.** *The retainer box prevents deflection on five sides of the urethane pad, causing the pad to deflect upward and around the punch radius or tip.*

no slippage between the workpiece and the pad. Slippage is common in standard steel tooling, which may or may not be a good thing, depending on the application.

## WORKING PARAMETERS

There are some ground rules that must be observed if this type of forming is to be done in a safe and functional manner. First, at the minimum, the urethane pad width must be twice the depth of penetration of the punch and workpiece combined.

Pad width (Pw) = punch penetration (Pp) × 2

Second, the urethane pad thickness should be a minimum of three times that of the punch and material penetration as shown in Figure 20-4.

Pad thickness (Pt) = punch penetration (Pp) × 3

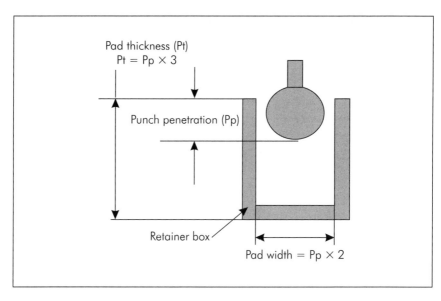

**Figure 20-4.** *At the minimum, the urethane pad width must be twice the depth of penetration of the punch and workpiece combined. The urethane pad thickness should be a minimum of three times that of the punch and material penetration.*

154

Third, the pad volume should be at least 10 times the volume of the penetrating punch and material.

Pad volume (Vp) = length $\times$ width $\times$ height

Punch volume (Pv) = $\pi \times$ (Mt. + Rp.)$^2 \times$ length

Working pad volume (Wv) $\geq$ Pv $\times$ 10

## Tonnage

As compared to a standard steel tool die set (air forming) urethane tonnage starts at three to five times that of air forming. This tonnage increases in direct proportion to an increase in the punch radius. In an attempt to decrease required tonnages, specialized pad shapes were developed for some specific styles of bend. In Figure 20-5, a U-bend is formed using a custom pad and deflection bars.

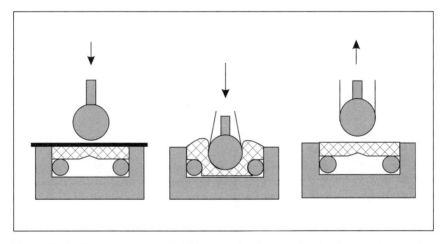

**Figure 20-5.** The progression of a U-bend, using both deflection bars and a molded pad. Note the small area of clearance at the bottom of the pad.

Because of the many variables, a true predictable tonnage is difficult, if not impossible, to determine. However, to get close to the required tonnage, the following formula works:

Tonnage per inch = ((575 $\times$ Mt.$^2$)/die width)$\times$ 12

True, this is the same formula as for the standard vee die. The width, however, is selected as the optimum die width for the radius and material described.

Urethane tonnage = tonnage per inch $\times$ 4

Working tonnage = urethane tonnage $\times$ workpiece length

### Air channel

For help in controlling the great pressures that can develop inside the pad and the retainer box, an air channel is sometimes provided as an area for the pad to flow, therefore minimizing the compressive strain (Figure 20-6). This channel is sometimes created by built-in deflection bars. Should your retainer box not have an air channel or built in deflection bars (smaller boxes normally do not have them), they should be created by the placement of free rolling deflection bars adjacent to the long sides of the retainer box. The diameter of these bars may be varied as necessary to achieve the desired results.

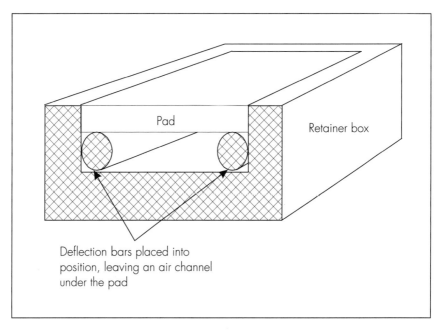

**Figure 20-6.** *To help in controlling great pressures that can develop inside the pad and the retainer box, an air channel is sometimes provided as an area for the pad to flow, minimizing compressive strain. This channel is sometimes created by built-in deflection bars.*

## Vee pads

Urethane also comes precut in a vee shape. It is designed to be placed into a standard vee die, allowing the vee to become the retainer box (Figure 20-7). This type of arrangement not only achieves a mar-free bend, but it is also capable of producing much smaller flange lengths than would be possible with a standard urethane pad. However, these

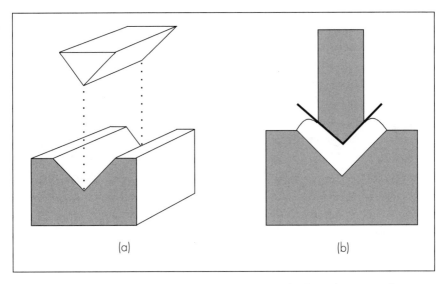

**Figure 20-7.** *Molded urethane pads that fit into a standard vee die are used in some special applications (a). In this case the vee die becomes the retainer box (b).*

short flanges (those less than three times the material thickness) can break past the surface tension of the urethane and cut down into the pad. If you need to use a urethane pad to form a small flange, sometimes a wrap of greater length will pull the bend into place without breaking into the urethane pad.

Die width selection for the vee/urethane combination is based on the urethane pad volume before anything else is considered.

### Hollow pads

A large variety of urethane dies with the air channel molded into the pad instead of the retainer box are available off the shelf. Some of these molded pads are channeled on both sides of the pad to help in extending the life of the pad. Molded urethane dies may be used in any type of retainer box, with or without deflection bars. Still, deflection bars are encouraged. It is this kind of molded or relieved pad and/or retainer box that allows for the 30 to 40 degrees of springback sometimes required for larger radius bends.

## Polydies

Polydies are a family of urethane tooling where the rectangular pad has holes of varying diameters placed through its full length. When the pad is collapsed it eliminates the need for deflection bars or air channels (Figure 20-8).

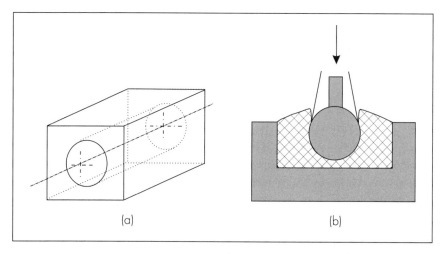

**Figure 20-8.** *Polydies have a rectangular pad containing holes of varying diameters (a). When the pad is collapsed, it eliminates the need for deflection bars or air channels (b).*

## Urethane Forming and Profound Radius Bending

Urethane dies offer some definite advantages over the standard steel vee die in forming a profound radius bend. The biggest advantage is entire elimination of the multi-breakage phenomenon, leaving an almost perfect bend radius every time. The difference between the finished workpiece radius and the measured punch radius is rarely more than 2% of the punch radius. This slight increase is caused by an unsatisfactory side pressure applied at the outside edge of the bend at the tangent points (Figure 20-9). This effect can be compensated for through the use of a molded urethane pad.

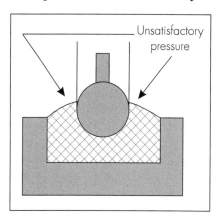

**Figure 20-9.** *Unsatisfactory pressure occurs in the urethane process only at the top two edges of the interaction of the pad and workpiece.*

## Nondeflecting Tools

This is the second group of tools created from urethane, the nondeflecting style. These dies, cast to shape from a very hard elastomer (plastic), come in the same sizes and shapes common to steel press brake tooling (Figure 20-10). They offer mar-free forming with a relatively long tool life, approximately 60,000 hits or bends. The only disadvantage with this type of tooling is that it may become impregnated with small bits of metal. At some point these begin to cause the same type of die marks common to standard steel tools. This, of course, will not hinder any forming where die marks or finishes are not a problem.

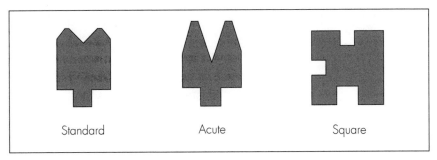

Standard          Acute          Square

**Figure 20-10.** *Urethane castings come in the same sizes and shapes common to steel press brake tooling.*

# Chapter 21

# MACHINE OPERATIONS

## MACHINE SETUPS

Most multi-axis press brakes have a high-speed ram approach. Primarily, the high-speed approach function is used to traverse the distance between the shut and open height, when the open height exceeds a safe distance for the removal of a workpiece from the machine (as was shown in Figure 5-1), thus increasing productivity.

### Up-acting Machines

With the ram at rest, it is relatively easy to hold the workpiece firmly against the backgages without using any pressure against the stops. However, when the high-speed approach is employed, a lot of movement takes place, not just with the ram.

As the ram takes off at high speed, you are left in the position of trying to catch up. When the ram slows down you are still moving at high speed. Now you have gone from trying to catch up to leading the ram. When the ram finally makes contact with the material, the workpiece is slammed down against the top of the die. This series of actions, depicted in Figure 21-1, results in the operator having to decide whether to let variations in dimension go or lean into (push against) the backgage to maintain the required dimension. Neither case is acceptable.

First, one slip and the operator could be between the punch and die as they close together.

The second reason is that, even with your pushing against the backgage, dimensional variations will still be apparent since you cannot apply consistent pressure each time you form a part. There is only a certain amount of running clearance built into the backgage system. Every time you push into the backgage, you use up a different amount of this clearance. As time and use take their toll on the machine, this error continues to increase.

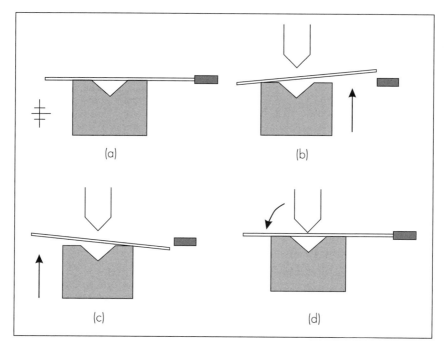

**Figure 21-1.** The high speed approach function: (a) ram at rest with workpiece relatively easy to hold; (b) ram takes off at high speed leaving operator to catch up; (c) ram slows down and now operator is leading; (d) ram makes contact with the material and workpiece is slammed down against top of die.

To demonstrate, attach a dial indicator to the press brake. Now, with some kind of probe attached to the backgage (Figure 21-2), try pushing against the backgage with your hand. See if you can get a consistent reading every time. It's not easy to do, no matter how deliberate you are.

The best way to avoid this situation is to keep the open height to a minimum. By using only the slower speeds and a light touch against the backgage/stops, a consistent bend dimension can be achieved. Even if the machine is a down-acting press break, the narrower the open height, the less likely the operator will be caught in the press.

If the press brake is of a mechanical type, where the open height is fixed, the best possible procedure is to cycle the ram past top dead center (TDC). Then, remove the finished piece, place the next piece in. Bring the ram down slowly and come to a complete stop above the material. Adjust the workpiece against the stops and slowly finish the bend, ending up just past top dead center. With a flywheel-driven machine the importance of not leaning into the backgage is even greater. Due to the

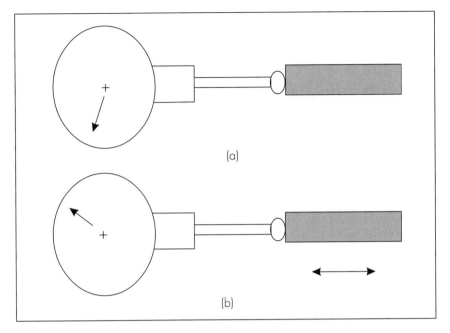

*Figure 21-2. After attaching a dial indicator to the press brake and resting it against the backgage (a), try to put the same pressure against the stops consistently (b). If the machine is not new, there is a good chance that it can't be done.*

large open height, the operator slipping into the press brake is a real possibility.

## TOOLING INSTALLATION

Regardless of the type of press brake being used, the ram needs to be in the "shut" position, with the ram at its full extension during tooling installation. If the machine being operated has adjustable distance pieces, be sure that these pieces have all been placed into their original settings. Then, as the machine is brought up to the "zeroing" point on the pressure gage, all the pieces will carry an equal load.

### Tool Staging

Staging refers to the use of multiple die sets, both like and unlike tooling types. It allows the operator to do more of each workpiece per setup. Figure 21-3 shows a staged tooling setup using similar sets of tools. An example would be using a 0.060 in. (1.524 mm) punch radius and 0.394 in. (10.008 mm) bottom die in all positions. In this case,

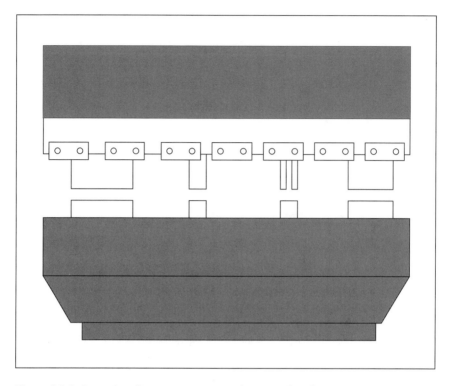

**Figure 21-3.** Staged tooling setup using similar sets of tools.

staging is only a matter of spacing the tooling out along the length of the bed.

Staging mismatched tooling is not quite as simple. Not only do we need to consider the spacing of the tooling left to right, but we also need to shim for height. Select the tooling that would be required to form the piece shown in Figure 21-4. Disregard that this particular piece could be formed using only an acute die set. The point of this section is to learn to mix and match tooling sets.

Laying the tooling you have selected in front of you, select and then measure the tallest. Depending on the application, you may need to include the height of the bolster and tool holder, as shown in Figure 21-5.

After you have decided which is the tallest set, install that set into the press brake in the prescribed manner. Once zeroing is completed, open the shut height a small amount and then lock the ram into position. Start with 0.020 in. (0.508 mm) or 0.030 in. (0.762 mm), you may need to open it up farther (Figure 21-6), enough to allow clearance for the next set of tooling. Now install the remaining tooling according to height and bring the machine back to zero pressure. The difference

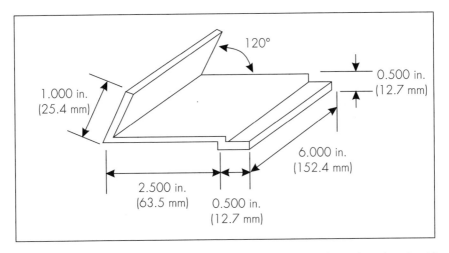

**Figure 21-4.** Staging tooling is not too difficult when it is all like tooling, but should you encounter a part like this one, it is not so easy. As you will see, it is still possible to stage this piece in a single setup.

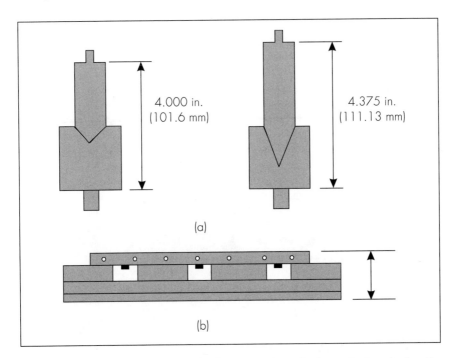

**Figure 21-5.** In shimming for height during staging of mismatched tools, lay the tooling in front of you and measure the tallest (a). You may need to include the height of the bolster and tooling holder (b).

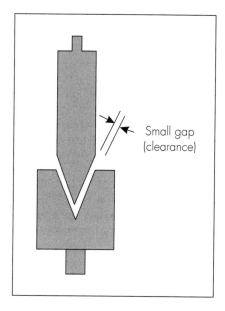

**Figure 21-6.** *The shut height might have to be opened farther to allow clearance for the next set of tooling.*

between the zeroed controller and the current controller reading is the amount of shim required to even the tooling.

If a direct reading from the controller is not available so that the shim height can be found (Figure 21-7), you may need to physically measure this distance. Once this amount has been found, place the shims above or below the tooling set as necessary, making safety your primary concern.

## Forming Order

After the shims have been placed in a safe position (preferably under the bolster in an up-acting machine, as is demonstrated in Figure 21-8) simply raise the tool holder just enough to firmly hold the bolster.

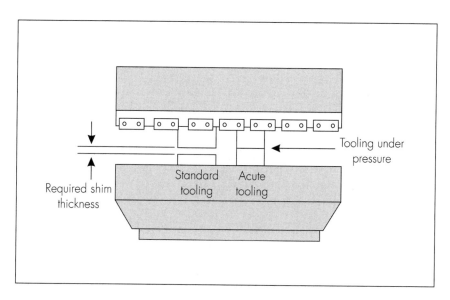

**Figure 21-7.** *The operator may need to measure the distance to find the correct shim height.*

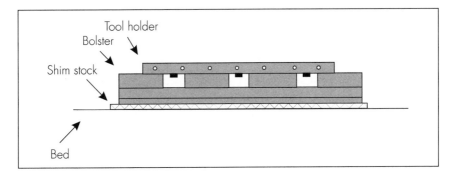

**Figure 21-8.** *After the shims are placed in a safe position, such as under the bolster, raise the tool holder enough to firmly hold the bolster.*

Once all of the tooling is in place, you need to re-zero the press brake controller again with the entire setup under pressure. Double check to make sure all the tooling is under pressure and no piece is left loose. When this has been accomplished, the machine is ready for programming.

The part displayed in Figure 21-4 would form something like Figure 21-9. By placing all tooling at a common zero point, not only will the programming be easier, but there is a diminished likelihood of a major crash from forming the right step in the wrong tool. It will occasionally happen, but the crash will be less severe.

Figure 21-9 is by no means the only order in which a piece may be formed. There is no set rule as to the best order in which to form a given part. Figure 21-10 depicts seven different orders that could be used to form this part. These orders are based on double wide precision ground dies, although any style of tooling will do just as well.

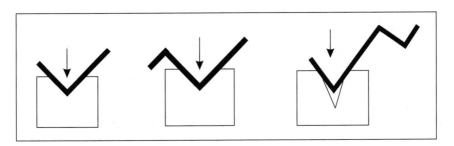

**Figure 21-9.** *This shows only one example of the order of forming that could be used to form the piece shown in Figure 21-4.*

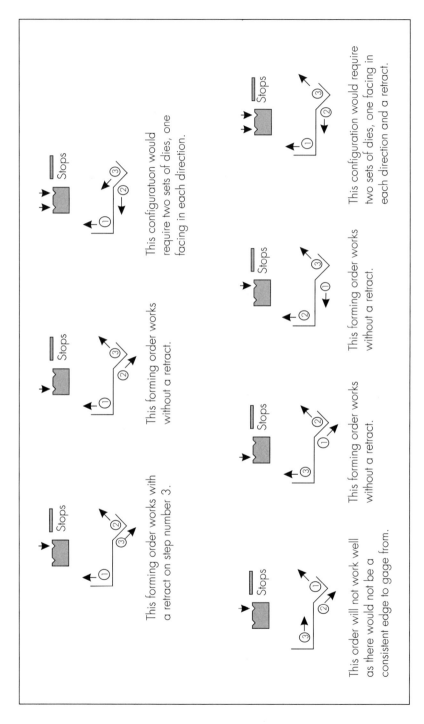

*Figure 21-10. Seven forming orders that could be used to form a part.*

The order of the drawings in Figure 21-10 is of no importance. Each of these is viable. Some may work better than others, but it comes down to whatever you find most comfortable.

Try to find the fastest and most efficient method for you. If it is easier to spin the piece to the left for the next bend, set it up that way. Be creative.

Another part of forming order concerns internal flanges. Many times you will be asked to form up a box or similar object that will have internal flanges that interfere with each other (Figure 21-11).

The order in which forming is to be accomplished during the bending of internal flanges obligates us to consider springback as the most important factor. Regardless of whether you are air forming, bottom bending, or coining, the material needs to pass by the required angle to achieve the correct bend angle when it is released.

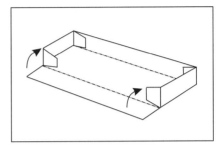

**Figure 21-11.** *If this piece were to be formed in this order, the final flange would interfere with the interval flanges because of springback.*

If this part were to be formed as shown in Figure 21-11, the side flange would encounter the ears from the end pieces.

This interference would cause the corners of the part to flare out because the material could not pass by the ears. On the other hand, if you reversed the order of forming on the last four bends, these ears would pass freely inside the side flanges, past 90 degrees, and up to the springback value.

# Chapter 22

# CREATIVE SOLUTIONS FOR COMMON PROBLEMS

In this chapter we look at several tricks of the trade for solving various bending problems.

## WINDOW PUNCHES

The "window" punch, can be created by using a standard punch with the use of distance pieces or by cutting and shimming a window in the punch. This is done to facilitate the bending of deep draw channels. Figure 22-1 shows examples of windows created by both methods.

Many times, when an object is formed the first bend comes out okay, but when the second bend is attempted, the first bend needs to pass through what is normally the punch or ram. If this final form is attempted, severe backbending occurs. However, when a window is incorporated into the setup, backbending can be avoided. An example is illustrated in Figure 22-2.

This may seem like a simple process, but there are some very tricky things that need to be considered.

### Tonnage

First to be considered is the tonnage. It should be apparent that a window punch is very weak at the center. The larger the span, the less tonnage the tool will handle. Therefore, it is recommended that air forming be the method of choice. Remember that bottom bending can increase the tonnage required by at least 150%, and coining requires as much as 100 times the pressure of air forming.

Air forming also lets you use the 20% rule to establish the bend radius through die width. As you open up the die width, the required pressure lowers accordingly.

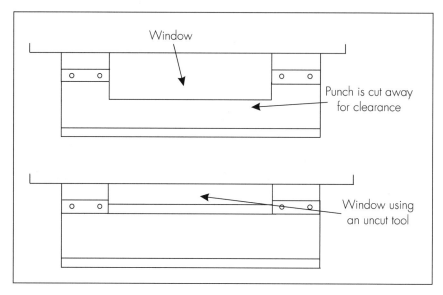

**Figure 22-1.** *A window can be created in a punch by cutting, or through the use of spacers.*

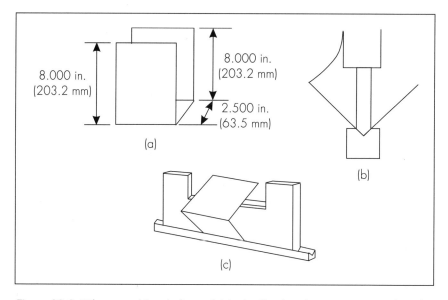

**Figure 22-2.** *When an object is formed (a), the first bend may come out okay, but the second may need to pass through what is normally the punch or ram. If this final form is attempted, severe backbending occurs (b). When a window is incorporated into the setup (c), backbending can be avoided.*

In the following examples please note the relationships between the inside radius (Ir), bend deduction (BD), and die width. Both are solutions to the same problem.

Standard tool set.

Mt. = 0.036 in. (0.914 mm)     BD = 0.0726 in. (1.844 mm)
Rp. = 0.060 in. (1.524 mm)     Optimum die width = 0.329 in.
∠   = 90 degrees                   (8.357 mm)
                                   Tonnage per in. = 0.3118 (5.6 MN)

The 20% rule applied.

Mt. = 0.036 in. (0.914 mm)     BD = 0.0769 in. (1.953 mm)
Rp. = 0.060 in. (1.524 mm)     Optimum die width = 0.472 in.
∠   = 90 degrees                   (11.989 mm)
Ir   = 0.070 in. (1.778 mm)     Tonnage per in. = 0.2173 (3.9 MN)

The comparison.

  0.070 in. (1.778 mm) Ir
– 0.060 in. (1.524 mm) Rp.
  0.010 in. (0.254 mm) Radius difference


  0.0769 in. (1.953 mm) BD at 0.070 Ir
– 0.0726 in. (1.844 mm) BD at 0.060 Ir
  0.0043 in. (0.109 mm) BD difference


  0.3118 Tonnage per in. (5.6 MN) for 0.329-in. (8.357-mm) bottom die
– 0.2173 Tonnage per in. (3.9 MN) for 0.472-in. (11.989-mm) bottom die
  0.0945 Tonnage per in. difference

Over 15 in. (381 mm), 0.0945 tons per in. (1.7 MN) would equal 1.41 tons (25.3 MN) of difference.

Why should we worry about such a small amount of tonnage? There are several reasons, with the first being that a window punch is not capable of spanning any great distance. Again, the wider span becomes, the weaker it is in the center.

## Shims

As a rule, when the forming process transpires, the punch will "flex" up across the entire length (Figure 22-3). Because of this flexing, one or more shims are required toward the center of the span to compensate for the flexing. As discussed in Chapter 15, the larger a die, the greater the number of shims required to effect one degree of change in bend angle.

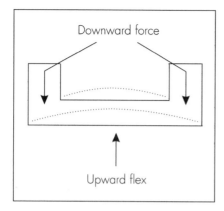

**Figure 22-3.** As the forming process transpires, the punch flexes up across the entire length of the window, and one or more shims are needed toward the span's center to compensate.

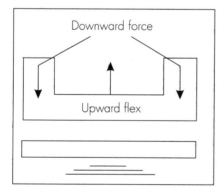

*Figure 22-4.* One way to reduce flexing in a window punch is to counterbalance the load. Note how the power flows through the tooling and where the flex will occur.

The window punch is the exception to this rule. Because of the very light tonnage abilities of a windowed punch, the use of a larger-than-normal die width eliminates the need for a considerable amount of shim. Why? Because:

1. The lighter the tonnage requirements, the less flexing motion.
2. The less flexing, the fewer number of shims required to compensate for any error.

There is still one more way to reduce the amount of flexing in a window punch—counterbalancing the load. Notice in Figure 22-4 how the power flows through the tooling and where the flex is going to occur. If, on the other hand, a small piece of the same material is placed at both ends of the punch, the flexing motion will be greatly reduced. This type of shimming can either lie in the bottom of the vee die or be double-back taped to the punch as shown in Figure 22-5.

Balancing the load also can be used across the entire length of the press brake bed. When a press brake is loaded to one side of the machine, it is common to encounter twist or shut down, just as in the case of the conventional press brake shown in Figure 22-6a.

To rectify the situation, place the correct amount of forming shims on the side of the press where there is no load. This will balance the load. However, the forming shims may not be thick enough to provide the exact balance needed. In that case, just a few—or even one—paper shims added to the workpiece may provide just the right bulk to balance the load perfectly (Figure 22-6b).

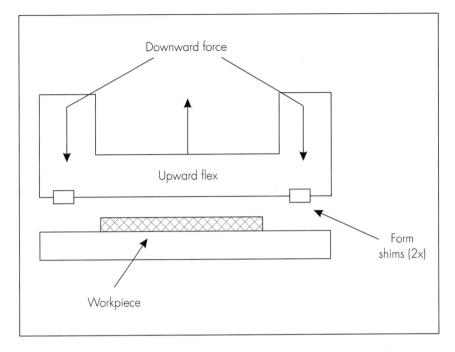

**Figure 22-5.** *Flexing motion can be greatly reduced if a small piece of the same material is placed at both ends of the punch. This type of shimming can either lie in the bottom of the vee die or be double-back taped to the punch.*

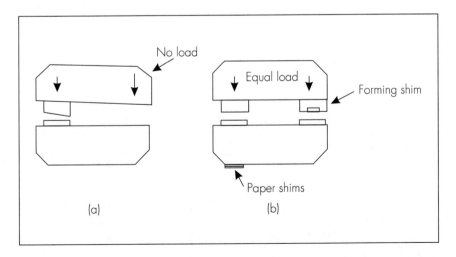

**Figure 22-6.** *When a load is unbalanced (a), the situation may be corrected by adding forming shims to the press and, if necessary, paper shims to the workpiece (b).*

## FORM GUSSETS

Form gussets are used to add strength to a bend. There is a right way and a wrong way to set up this type of forming method, whose object is to allow the material to flow just a little. When the clearance is too tight, the gusset will tear through and actually end up weakening the bend, rather than strengthening it (Figure 22-7).

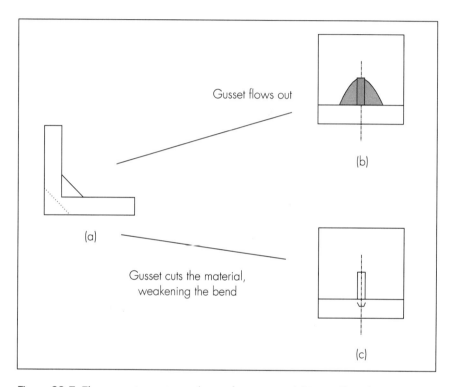

**Figure 22-7.** *The correct way to produce a form gusset (a) is to allow the material to flow out from the gusset (b). If the gusset clearance is too small, the material tends to shear, which weakens the overall gusset (c).*

The formed gusset is best produced by placing a piece of material (preferably stainless steel) between two die pieces. Rarely is it ever a critical feature as far as location is concerned. It commonly uses the largest of allowable tolerances, which works in your favor when it comes to selecting the punch and die.

To produce the flowing effect, a small-piece shim is added to either side of the gusset. Also, a thin strip of stainless steel is placed along the top of the bed on which the dies and gusset are placed. This keeps the gusset from imbedding itself into the bolster during the forming process. Make sure this shim runs the entire length of the tooling to maintain a common plane (Figure 22-8).

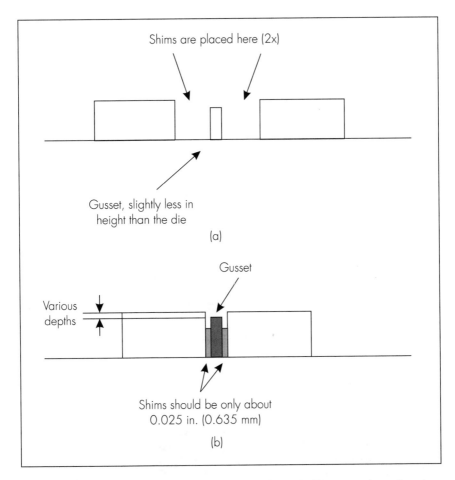

**Figure 22-8.** *The gusset is placed between two dies (a). Shims are then placed on either side of the gusset to regulate the amount of material flow (b).*

## CARRYING A BEND OR CREATIVE DIE SPACING

Many times the exact length of the required tooling is unavailable. For example, if you have a workpiece measuring 6.087 in. (154.6 mm) along the length of the bend, and the next largest die set is too long, multiple pieces of tooling are needed. In this case, total die length only adds up to 6.000 in. (152.4 mm). This means that 0.087 in. (2.21 mm) must be compensated for through the use of spacing.

While it does not apply to all circumstances, it is generally best to carry the bend somewhere in the center rather than to the outside of the bend. When the ends are not supported, they tend to "blow out." The severity of this kind of oversight varies according to the punch radius and die width. However, when the excess bend length is spread out across the length of the die, both ends are supported, and the bend is carried without a blowout. The full length of the bend should have a smooth outside surface. However, some distortion may occur in the center if the span becomes too great (Figure 22-9).

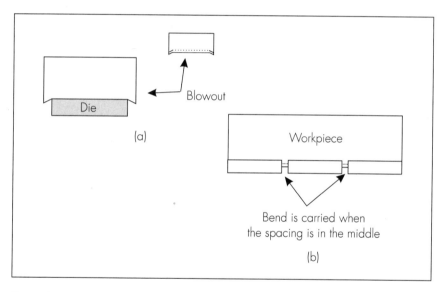

**Figure 22-9.** *When the workpiece ends are not supported, they tend to blow out (a). However, when the excess bend is spread out across the length of the die, both ends are supported and the bend is carried without a blowout (b).*

## FORMING WRAPS

Often a workpiece may have a hole or feature that lies within the area described by the outside setback (OSSB). Within this area, distortion of the feature occurs and worsens as the feature approaches the bend line. This distortion can, partially if not totally, be stopped through the use of forming wraps, such as wipes, double form strips, and back-ups, all of which perform the same function.

Selecting the correct material thickness of the wrap is critical to this process. To begin, place the outside surface of the workpiece at forty four one hundredths of the combined total thickness of the workpiece and the wrap. This puts the outside surface of the workpiece where it will encounter the least natural material deformation. As you may recall, forty four one hundredths is the neutral axis, where no change in the material occurs during forming. Of course, this is not a solid piece of material, so some distortion is going to occur.

Material thickness = 0.046 in. (1.168 mm)
Wrap thickness    = 0.060 in. (1.524 mm)

The total here is 0.106 in. (2.692 mm). Forty four one hundredths of 0.106 is 0.046 in. (1.168 mm), as close to perfect as you could possibly hope. The die width for this type of bend also should be selected on the basis of the combined total of wrap and material thickness.

## SQUARING THE STOPS

When looking at the relationship of the punch and die set to the backgage, it is important to look at it as a triangle. If you have a taper in the flange that you just formed, for example ten thousandths, you could shim the heavy side back to square or just shift the stops to the right or left, depending on the particular problem. By shifting one stop or the other, you can change the triangular relationship to the bend line. Figure 22-10 depicts this concept. Of course, this works well only with the more subtle tapers; larger ones still require shimming.

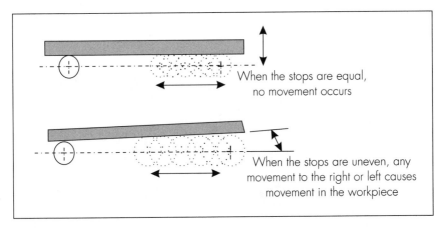

When the stops are equal, no movement occurs

When the stops are uneven, any movement to the right or left causes movement in the workpiece

**Figure 22-10.** By shifting one of the stops, the operator can change the triangular relationship to the bend line.

# Chapter 23

# GAGING

## SIDE GAGING

There are times when side gaging becomes necessary. This type of gaging can be very accurate and consistent once it is established as a setup. Figure 23-1 shows two examples of side gaging that would be of great value in forming.

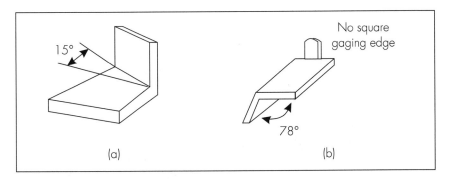

**Figure 23-1.** *The side gaging examples shown here are two of several possibilities. Item (a) requires a side gage attached to the back of the die. Where (b) shows a workpiece that could be produced by gaging off the side of the die itself.*

There are only two basic types of side gaging. The first type is where the gage is clamped in some manner to the die body or to the bed of the press brake (Figure 23-2). Generally, the gage is mounted to a table and then C-clamped to the die, which is then mounted into the press brake. You can create a second type of side gage by using the side of the die as your straight edge. This approach, however, has a unique problem—the inside radius of the previous bend.

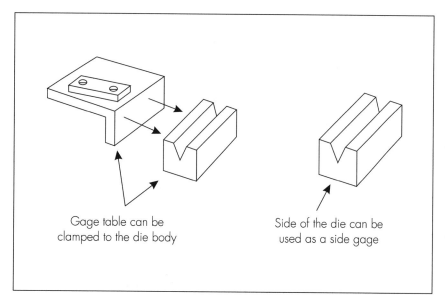

**Figure 23-2.** *In one type of side gaging, the gage is clamped to the die body or to the bed of the press brake. In some cases, the side of the die may be used as a side gage.*

The problem is that the radius rides up on the die causing wide variations in both the squareness of the second bend and its dimension. It also causes the first bend angle, the one being gaged from, to be opened back up to a different bend angle.

There is a simple way to solve this problem. Add a piece of material with a thickness greater than or equal to the inside setback (ISSB) of the part to be gaged. This shim can be attached to the die by means of strong glue or double-backed tape (Figure 23-3). With the addition of this shim, the first flange now lies flat against the die and, therefore, square to the bend line.

One last note about gaging from the second bend. Look closely at any piece of material that has been formed, the thicker the better for the sake of this explanation. Notice that there is a convex blowout on one edge of the bend and a concave area on the other (Figure 23-4). If you try to gage from the side with the convex blowout you will have either a rocking motion or, at least, inconsistent angular changes. This concave/convex condition occurs regardless of the material thickness or bend radius. But it does increase in direct proportion to an increase in either thickness or radius. This must be a consideration when you are figuring out a forming order before the first piece is run.

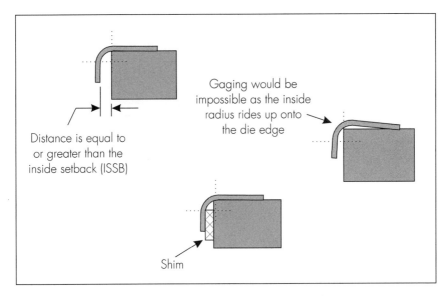

**Figure 23-3.** *When gaging is done using the side of the die, a unique problem occurs: riding up into the radius of the previous bend. By placing a shim that is equal to or greater than the inside setback (ISSB), the workpiece is assured a square and firm edge to gage from.*

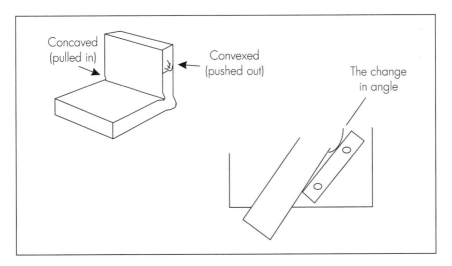

**Figure 23-4.** *When side gaging, the concave/convex edges must be taken into account. All material that is formed will develop this feature, one on each end of the bend. Should you try to use the edge with the concaved bend, some angular adjustment may be needed to maintain a good angle.*

183

# Chapter 24

# PIN GAGING

## WHAT IS PIN GAGING?

There are times when workpieces cause problems, due to either an extra tight edge-to-feature tolerance or a lack of square edges (Figure 24-1). These two problems have a common solution, pin gages. These are usually no more than just long pieces of material (plastic, metal, etc.) attached to the backgage, with a small pin located close to the end.

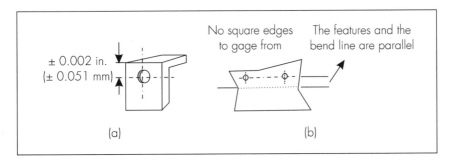

**Figure 24-1.** Workpieces can cause problems because of extra tight edge-to-feature tolerance (a) or a lack of square edges (b).

The trick to using a pin gage is in the way you actually gage against it. Looking at Figure 24-2, which side of the hole or feature would you gage from? Does it matter? Yes, it does matter. If the pin were placed against the back of the hole or feature, the feature or hole would not clear the pin as it begins to rise up during forming.

On the other hand, if you gaged off the front of the hole or feature, the workpiece lifts off the pin with ease, assuming that the pin is not too tall. As a general rule, the height of the pin should not exceed that of the

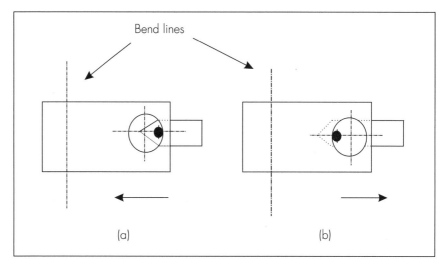

*Figure 24-2.* When gaging with a pin gage the feature edge to be gaged from is of great importance. Both views show the same workpiece in relationship to the bend line. Which is the correct way to gage this part? In (a) the workpiece would not clear the pin; (b), on the other hand, would clear the pin during forming. By gaging from the inside side of the feature (the edge nearest the bend line) the back edge lifts up and over the pin.

feature size less the diameter of the pin. Figures 24-3a and b show the relationship of the pin height to hole diameter during the forming of a 90-degree bend. This can be mathematically expressed in the following manner:

Feature width or hole diameter – pin diameter = maximum pin height

Figure 24-3c represents how this measurement is made.

## Gaging from a Negative Position

When you are gaging from a notch or pin holes located at zero (the bend line) or less, as shown in Figure 24-4, it is like gaging off the wrong side of the feature. The easiest way to deal with this problem is to retract the backgage just enough to allow clearance of the workpiece.

## Retracting

Retracting the backgage is, for the most part, unnecessary as most press brakes have stops designed to flip out of the way. If you want to complete the forming of a reverse bend without using the retract function, the location of the stop to the flange is very important. Note that in Figure 24-5a the stop is not located so low as to cause interference as the bend forms up. In Figure 24-5b the stop is set so that it rests within

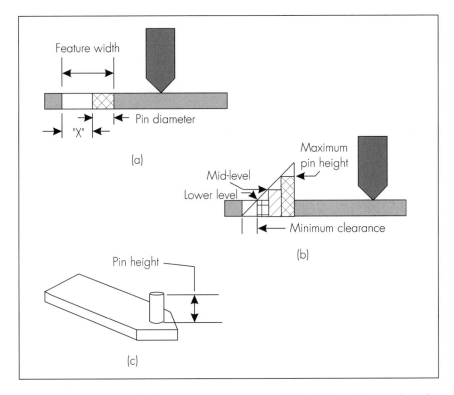

**Figure 24-3.** *The size of the pin is very important if the pin is going to clear the workpiece. Views (a) and (b) show this relationship. The pin height is measured in the manner described in view (c).*

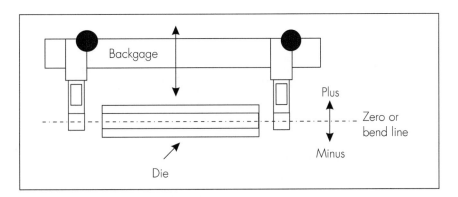

**Figure 24-4.** *Gaging from a notch or pin holes located at zero or less is like gaging off the wrong side of the feature. You can deal with the problem by simply retracting the backgage enough to allow the workpiece to clear.*

the area described by the outside setback. In this location, the stop flips up out of the way effortlessly. This also allows a firm surface to gage from. Don't use the retract function unless absolutely necessary, or it will just waste time.

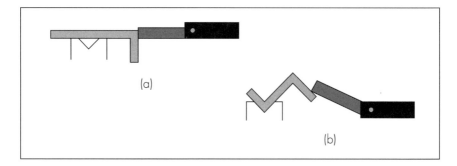

**Figure 24-5.** *To complete the forming of a reverse bend without using the retract function, location of the stop to the flange is important. The stop is not located so low that it causes interference as the bend forms up (a). Or the stop can be set so that it rests within the area described by the outside setback (b) and it flips effortlessly out of the way.*

# Chapter 25

# DEEP BOX FORMING

Is this box too deep to form? This is one of the most common and difficult problems you will encounter.

The first step is to find the total clearance required to form a given part. You could consult a chart such as the one shown in Figure 25-1. There is, however, a better and more accurate way to develop this information. Look closely at Figure 25-2a to see the two right-angle triangles. They both have the centerline of the punch in common.

Figure 25-2b shows the same triangles with the punch removed for clarity. Assuming that the angle is less than 90 degrees and you are using a standard balanced tool (45 degrees on a side) and a box depth of 10.000 in. (25.4 cm), the first triangle is solved as follows:

$C$ = 14.142 in. (35.92 cm)
$c$ = 90 degrees
$B$ = 10.000 in. (25.4 cm)
$b$ = 45 degrees
$A$ = 10.000 in. (25.4 cm)
$a$ = 45 degrees

This alone does not allow enough clearance to form the part, so we need to solve for the second triangle. To solve this triangle we need to decide

| Box depth | Minimum punch height |
|-----------|----------------------|
| 1 | 2 3/4 |
| 1 1/2 | 3 15/32 |
| 2 | 4 3/16 |
| 2 1/2 | 4 29/32 |
| 3 | 5 19/32 |
| 3 1/2 | 6 5/16 |
| 4 | 7 |
| 4 1/2 | 7 23/32 |
| 5 | 8 13/32 |
| 5 1/2 | 9 1/8 |
| 6 | 9 27/32 |
| 6 1/2 | 10 17/32 |
| 7 | 11 1/4 |
| 7 1/2 | 11 31/32 |
| 8 | 12 21/32 |
| 8 1/2 | 13 3/8 |
| 9 | 14 1/16 |
| 9 1/2 | 14 25/32 |
| 10 | 15 1/2 |

**Figure 25-1.** *A standard chart used to develop the information about a box depth, as well as the minimum tooling clearances required to perform this operation.*

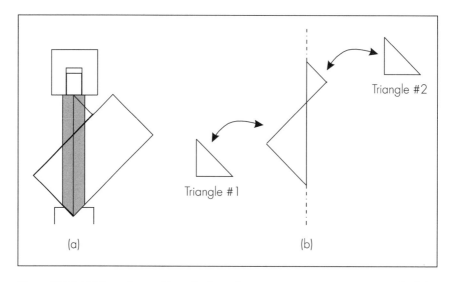

**Figure 25-2.** *While a chart will work okay, there are more accurate ways to find the total required clearance. View (a) shows the two triangles that describe the tool height; (b) shows the same two triangles with the tool removed.*

what we know about it. First we know that angles *b* and *a* are 45 degrees and angle *c* is 90 degrees. So to solve it, we only need one more piece of information. The dimension from any side will do. There are many ways we could arrive at the answer, but the easiest is to measure the ram and divide the answer by two.

Because angles *b* and *a* are 45 degrees, and we know that one half of the ram is equal to sides *B* and *A* of the triangle (in this case, side *C* is irrelevant), and the ram is 2.500 in. (63.5 mm), then side *B* or *A* is 1.250 in. (31.75 mm). We still need to allow for springback, so, instead of dividing the ram by two, just multiply by 0.563. This could allow enough springback clearance to form the part, meaning the minimum required tool height could be expressed as:

Flange depth = *B*
Tool angle (45 degrees) = *b*
Ram width = Rw
Allowable minimum height = (*B*/cosine *b*) + (Rw × 0.563)

If additional clearance is needed, it could be provided through the use of a 30/60 unbalanced punch and die (Figure 25-3). Figure 25-4 shows two charts, one balanced and one unbalanced for a side-by-side comparison.

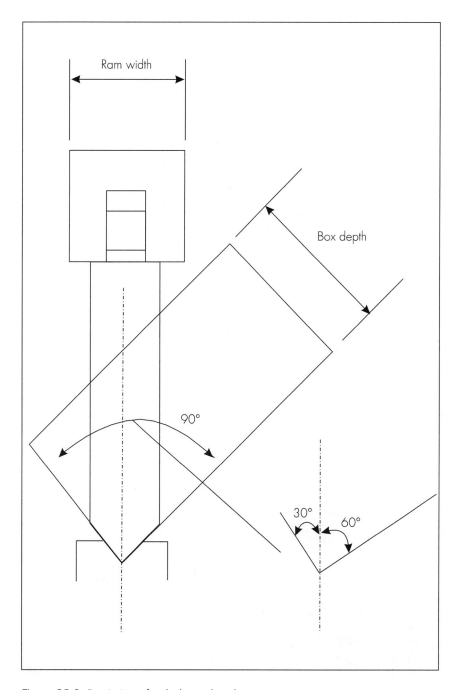

**Figure 25-3.** Depiction of unbalanced tool set.

| Box depth | Minimum punch height | Box depth | Minimum punch height |
|-----------|---------------------|-----------|---------------------|
| 1 | 2 3/4 | 1 | 1 15/16 |
| 1 1/2 | 3 15/32 | 1 1/2 | 2 17/32 |
| 2 | 4 3/16 | 2 | 3 3/32 |
| 2 1/2 | 4 29/32 | 2 1/2 | 3 11/16 |
| 3 | 5 19/32 | 3 | 4 1/4 |
| 3 1/2 | 6 5/16 | 3 1/2 | 4 27/32 |
| 4 | 7 | 4 | 5 13/32 |
| 4 1/2 | 7 23/32 | 4 1/2 | 6 |
| 5 | 8 13/32 | 5 | 6 9/16 |
| 5 1/2 | 9 1/8 | 5 1/2 | 7 7/32 |
| 6 | 9 27/32 | 6 | 7 23/32 |
| 6 1/2 | 10 17/32 | 6 1/2 | 8 5/16 |
| 7 | 11 1/4 | 7 | 8 7/8 |
| 7 1/2 | 11 31/32 | 7 1/2 | 9 15/32 |
| 8 | 12 21/32 | 8 | 10 1/32 |
| 8 1/2 | 13 3/8 | 8 1/2 | 10 5/8 |
| 9 | 14 1/16 | 9 | 11 3/16 |
| 9 1/2 | 14 25/32 | 9 1/2 | 11 25/32 |
| 10 | 15 1/2 | 10 | 12 11/32 |

| 90-degree punches and dies | 30/60-degree punch and die set |
|:---:|:---:|
| (a) | (b) |

**Figure 25-4.** *Two charts, one balanced (a) and the other unbalanced (b). Note the substantial rise in possible height of bends that can be produced.*

The method that we would use to solve for an unbalanced tool is the same as it would be for a standard 45-degree balanced tool. The top triangle is still a 45-degree right-angle triangle and the rest is solved as before. With the unbalanced tool, the only part of the formula that changes is angle $a$; everything else is still the same.

This means that the minimum required tool height can be expressed as:

Flange depth = $B$
Tool angle (30 degrees) = $a$
Ram width = Rw
Allowable minimum height = $(B/\text{cosine } a) + (\text{Rw} \times 0.563)$

# Chapter 26

# RELATED EQUIPMENT

## SLIP ROLLER

The sole purpose of slip rollers is to roll sheet metal either to flatten it or roll it into a cylinder. They are used to produce cones and large radius bends. Slip rollers come in a large variety of roll diameters and roll lengths, and may be hand or motor driven, depending on size and capacity.

The traditional slip roller consists of three rollers, which, if adjusted properly, remove or add a radius to the material being worked.

As the material is fed into the rollers, it first passes through the first two pinch rollers that hold the material during the rolling process. The third roller then forces the material upwards.

Another style of slip roller is the double-roll slip roller, with only two rollers, one urethane coated and one plain metal. It has a bending roll that can modify a workpiece's diameter. Two types of slip rollers are shown in Figure 26-1.

### Terms

Before we can continue, there are some terms with which you must become familiar.

**Breaking the sheet**. Pre-rolling a flat piece of material to relieve surface tension in the material (unflat) before a standard forming process.

**Cutouts**. Any opening in the workpiece: squares, rounds, etc.

**Fluting**. Freestanding variations in a radius after rolling.

**Free diameter.** The measured diameter or radius as it stands in an unrestrained state.

**In-the-air bending**. This is a term specific to the three-roll process. It refers to the fact that the workpiece is not captivated as the rolling operation is completed.

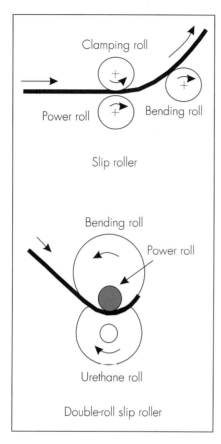

Clamping roll

Power roll

Bending roll

Slip roller

Bending roll

Power roll

Urethane roll

Double-roll slip roller

*Figure 26-1. Shown here are the two basic types of slip rollers. Both have a power roll that drives the material, a bending roll that puts the actual bend into the part, and a clamping roll (also known as a urethane roll) that the power rollers push against.*

**Kinking.** Blowout that occurs at the edges of a cutout or feature after rolling.

**Pinch type of slip roller.** A machine for roll-forming that uses only two rolls, with the radius produced by pinching pressure between the two rolls.

**Pyramid style of slip roller.** A roll-forming machine with three rollers that form a pyramid. The workpiece passes through the first two rollers (acting as the drivers) and then the third roller, which forces the workpiece upwards into a radius.

**Roll bending.** Bending a sheet metal part by passing it through a set of rollers.

## Three-roll Slip Roller

The three-roll slip roller can be broken down into two different subgroups, pyramid three-roll and three-roll pinch (Figure 26-2).

With the three-roll style, the material to be rolled is never confined by the roll itself, making this an in-the-air method of rolling a radius.

While this type of slip roller is an excellent machine for prototype work or short-run parts, in many cases the workpiece will need to pass between the rollers more than once, followed by an adjustment after each pass. This makes a specific diameter or radius tolerance difficult to maintain, the main reason why a three-roll slip roller is not a good machine for a long production run.

## Two-roll Slip Roller

Two-roll machines use a urethane-covered roller on the bottom and a steel top roller that is power driven by a center driver roll and capable of producing various diameters. Because of urethane's ability to act as a liquid under pressure, it forces the workpiece against the steel roll's radius, rather than just being pinched by the rolls.

The two-roll method of rolling is a captive system. From the time the material enters the roll, the forming process takes place (Figure 26-3).

In contrast, with the three-roll method, a short flat is produced in advance of the forming roll (Figure 26-4). By design, the two-roll slip roller can be set to roll a workpiece complete in just one pass. Under normal circumstances, no second operation is required. This makes it an excellent machine for long-running jobs or those jobs with tighter radius tolerances.

Because of urethane's liquid-like abilities, the springback normally within any material is relieved,

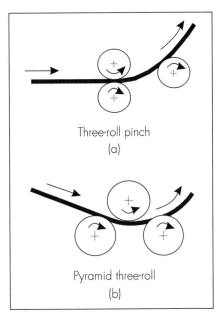

Three-roll pinch
(a)

Pyramid three-roll
(b)

**Figure 26-2.** *The three-roll slip roller is categorized into two subgroups, three-roll pinch (a) and pyramid three-roll (b).*

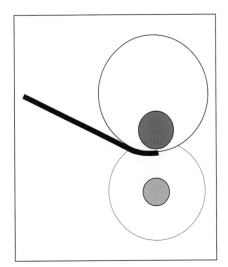

**Figure 26-3.** *In the two-roll method, the forming process begins as soon as the material enters the roll.*

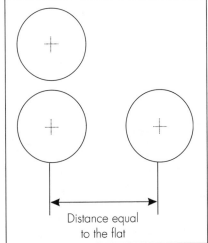

Distance equal
to the flat

**Figure 26-4.** *With the two-roll method, a short flat is produced in advance of the forming rolls.*

allowing a much higher standard of tolerance within the freestanding workpiece.

## Rolling Calculations

As stated earlier, the two-roll style begins the process the moment the material comes in contact with the rolls. This means that the flat blank size or feature location can be found directly.

The three-roll style, on the other hand, develops a short flat at each end of the radius. There are three different ways that this flat can be taken care of (Figure 26-5), that may or may not affect the outcome of the flat blank size or feature location. One way is to add material to both ends of the workpiece to increase the flat blank size that will later be resheared before the final roll is completed. You could also bend the roll in a standard press brake before the rolling process. This method allows

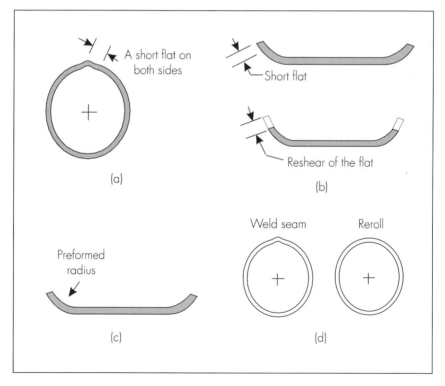

**Figure 26-5.** *In view (a) the short flat is described in the rolled part. View (b) shows one method to remove this flat, accomplished by reshearing the flat (assuming you allowed for it). View (c) shows the same problem solved by preforming the piece in a standard die set. Or, the part could be rerolled after welding (d).*

you to use exact shear sizes and feature locations. It is recommended that this pre-bend be completed in a standard vee die backed up with a urethane filler to help maintain a true radius. If the urethane backup is unavailable, the pre-bend punch radius should be a slightly smaller bend radius, air-formed in a standard vee die.

The third method uses an exact shear size to produce the final piece. This is accomplished by doing the initial rolling process, welding the seam and the reroll, then piecing to remove the two flats. The drawback to this method is that some kinking or fluting takes place around the welded area.

### Flat blank calculations

The flat blank of a rolled workpiece is solved in the same manner as any other bend radius. The length of the blank is computed along the neutral axis of the material at forty four one hundredths of the material thickness. This bend allowance (BA) is the flat length of the radius regardless of the degree of angle (Figure 26-6). The formula for computing this length is:

Bend allowance (BA) = ((0.017453 × Rp.) + (0.0078 × Mt.)) × ∠

Once the length of the flat blank has been computed, extra material would then be added to make the final part practical for you to roll.

### Operations

Before the rolling process begins, a process called "breaking the sheet" should be performed. The purpose of this process is to flatten a workpiece before it is rolled.

This procedure relieves all surface tension in the material, allowing better control over the freestanding dimensions in the finished piece. It also provides the ability to hold much tighter feature tolerances.

In breaking the sheet, the blank is fed through the rollers under very slight pressure, flipped, and then rolled again (Figure 26-7a). Along with relieving surface tension, variances in both the springback and the radius are

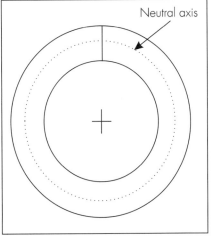

**Figure 26-6.** A flat blank calculation is computed along the neutral axis of the material at forty-four one hundredths of the material thickness. This bend allowance is the flat length of the radius regardless of the degree of angle.

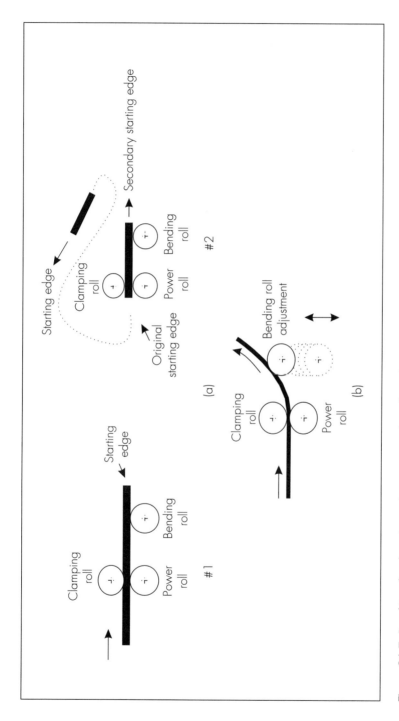

**Figure 26-7.** Breaking the sheet is used to remove a bow from the material before forming in the standard tool set. The workpiece is fed through first one way then flipped and fed a second time from the other end (a). View (b) shows the adjustment of the forming roll as it relates to the roll in the workpiece.

greatly reduced. Breaking the sheet is particularly important to the operator using the three-roll slip roller. Once the workpiece has been broken, setting up the desired angle and radius can then be fine tuned. This is done by the trial and error method, raising or lowering the third roller to produce the required radius or diameter (Figure 26-7b). The only other limiting factors, besides the length of the third roll, is the diameter of the roll itself and the maximum gage of material a given machine will roll. General length of the roll, gage of material, and roll diameter are given in Table 26-1.

**Table 26-1. General Parameters for Breaking the Sheet**

| Length | Maximum Gage | Roll Diameter |
|---|---|---|
| 6.000 in. (152.4 mm) | 16 gage | 1.000 in. (25.4 mm) |
| 12.000 in. (304.8 mm) | 16 gage | 2.000 in (50.8 mm) |
| 24.000 in. (609.6 mm) | 14 gage | 3.000 in. (76.2 mm) |
| 36.000 in. (914.4 mm) | 14 gage | 4.000 in. (101.6 mm) |

Note that the roll diameter must be smaller than the radius or diameter that you are trying to achieve (Figure 26-8). Each machine should have a tag located somewhere on the slip roll with the specifics for that machine.

Removing a finished 360-degree roll-formed part from the slip roll is accomplished through the use of a cam and lever, built into every roller. The roller lifts the top roll (Figure 26-9) after the clamping mechanism has been released.

Once the workpiece is removed from the roll, check for taper in the freestanding measured radius/diameter. Figure 26-10 shows which

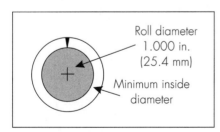

**Figure 26-8.** The roll diameter must be smaller than the radius or diameter you are trying to achieve.

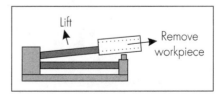

**Figure 26-9.** Removing a finished 360-degree roll-formed part from the slip roll is accomplished with a cam and lever. The roller lifts the top roll after the clamping mechanism has been released.

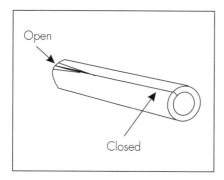

**Figure 26-10.** *Once the workpiece is removed from the roll, check for taper in the freestanding measured radius/diameter to see which side of the slip roll to adjust to achieve a uniform roll or diameter.*

side of the slip roll to adjust, up or down, to achieve a uniform roll or diameter.

## Cones

There are basically four different types of cones you will encounter from time to time in the precision sheet metal shop. The cones are: right, oblique, frustum, and truncated (Figure 26-11). Both the right and the oblique cones are considered to be closed. The frustum and truncated cones are open, meaning that the cone is not rolled together at the tangent point.

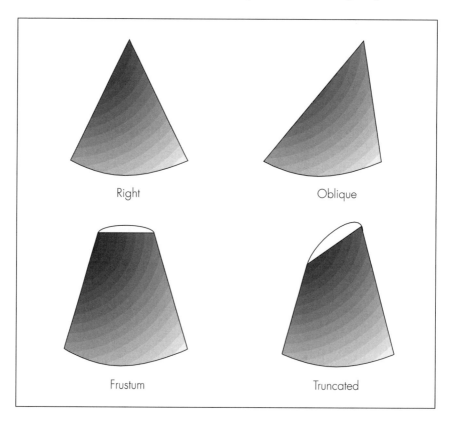

**Figure 26-11.** *The four types of cones.*

The right and oblique cones could never really be completely rolled due to the lack of an opening at the top. An opening being equal to or greater than the body of the roll enables the roll to be rolled. Because rolling is not possible with these types, the cone would have to be faked. Therefore, we only look at the open-style cones. A closed-style cone is best done in either a spinning or stamping process.

The difference between the truncated and frustum cones relates to the angle between the top and bottom planes. In the case of the frustum cone, the two cutting planes pass through the cone parallel to each other. The truncated cone has at least one plane occurring at any angle, except the one that would produce parallel cutting planes. Figure 26-12 shows the layout of a standard frustum cone.

### Cone rolling theory

Truncated and frustum cones are easy to roll form. The theory in cone rolling is that the inner radius and the outer radius must pass through the rollers at the same time. As seen in Figure 26-13a, the proportions of the flat blank are quite different from end to end; it is enhanced with dotted lines. As each section "A" of the workpiece passes through, a much larger section of material must pass through the rollers. At any given time the length of the roll will remain consistent if the roll is started square to the rollers. Only slight additional pressure to the larger end of the blank is necessary, and only to help the roll along. This firm, but consistent, pressure helps increase the rate at which the material passes through the rollers (Figure 26-13b). Loosening the pinch on the large end of the driving roll helps too.

## Wire Forming

A metal bar, tube, or rod also may be rolled. Although not limited to lighter gages and sizes, heavier materials require special equipment to roll form. In most cases, any wire forming done in a precision sheet metal shop will be performed with lighter gage materials.

Commonly, a groove or channel is cut into the rollers. These are shaped to accommodate a given product. It also should be noted that the flat size estimate can still be calculated around the neutral axis of the workpiece.

In the case of round stock, both the power roller and the clamping roller must be grooved. This keeps distortion and flattening of the material to a minimum. With square or box tubing the opposite is true, only the power roll needs to be relieved to accommodate the material to be rolled (Figure 26-14). Removing the finished workpiece is done in the same manner as with any part, by unclamping and then lifting the top roll.

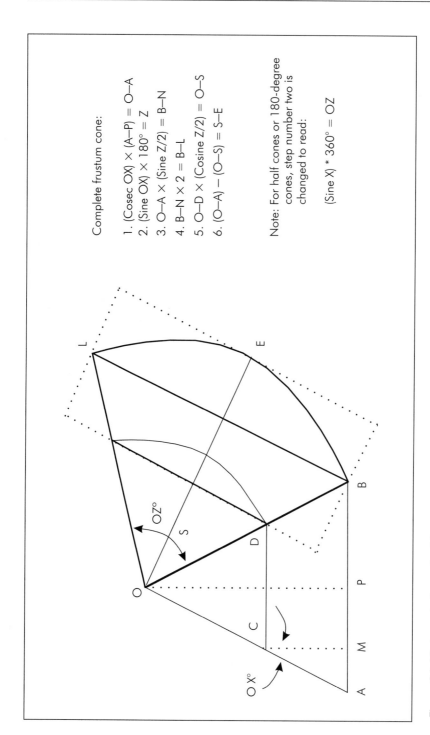

Complete frustum cone:

1. (Cosec OX) × (A–P) = O–A
2. (Sine OX) × 180° = Z
3. O–A × (Sine Z/2) = B–N
4. B–N × 2 = B–L
5. O–D × (Cosine Z/2) = O–S
6. (O–A) – (O–S) = S–E

Note: For half cones or 180-degree cones, step number two is changed to read:

(Sine X) * 360° = OZ

**Figure 26-12.** *Layout of standard frustum cone.*

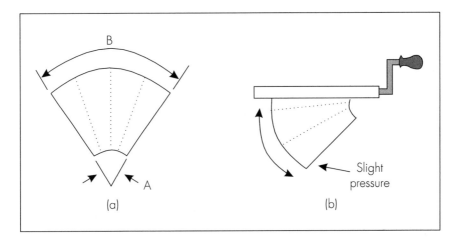

**Figure 26-13.** One consideration when rolling a cone is the fact that one side of the part is much longer than the other (a). To roll a cone correctly, slight pressure is needed to increase the flow of material through the rollers on the part's larger side (b).

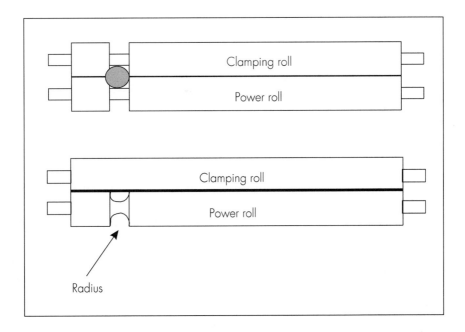

**Figure 26-14.** In wire forming, a groove or channel is cut into the rollers and shaped to accommodate a given product. With round stock, both the power roller and clamping roller are grooved. However, with square or box tubing, only the power roll must be relieved to accommodate the material to be rolled.

## General Slip Rolling Tips

Here are some tips to remember when slip rolling.

First, adjusting the clamping roll should be done in equal amounts after the rolls are parallel to each other. This goes for the "pinch" or "driving" rolls as well as the forming roll. If you always begin with this procedure, there will be far less trouble achieving, and then maintaining, consistent and accurate parts.

Second, never try to back a workpiece out of the slip roll (except in an emergency) while the rollers are still clamped into place. The workpiece is still being rolled regardless of the roll's direction. This will cause the radius to vary during the distance traveled by the roller. If it becomes necessary to remove a workpiece from the slip roller before completion of the roll, first lift the top roll. Make all adjustments and return the workpiece to complete the rolling.

Most important is safety! The following rule should always be obeyed: *Never wear loose clothing, gloves, or a necktie near a running slip roller!*

The slip roller is no more forgiving than a standard press brake and can inflict harm.

# Chapter 27

# THE LEAF BRAKE

For the most part, the hand-operated leaf brake is limited to use with 16-gage material with bend length limited only by the length of the forming beam. The most common sizes for hand-operated leaf brakes are: 6-in. (15.24 cm), 12-in. (30.48 cm), 24-in. (60.96 cm) and 36-in. (91.44 cm). There are only a few types of bends that a leaf brake cannot perform; and it does some better than a regular press brake.

## COMPOSITION OF THE LEAF BRAKE

Also known by such names as the box brake, hand brake, box and pan, and finger brake, the leaf brake consists of a main housing, forming bar, front leaf assembly, and clamping mechanism. The main housing is most commonly manufactured out of cast iron because of its durability and strength. Into this casting is machined a large flat area known as the "platen," as well as various mounting features required to assemble the brake.

The forming bar, attached to the main housing body, is lever-activated and cam-driven. When engaged, it becomes the clamping mechanism, holding the material in place during the forming process. Not only does the forming bar hold the material down, it uses the tooling to do it. In other words, it is also the tooling holder.

This tooling, or "fingers" as they are commonly called, comes in a variety of radii, tooling angles, and lengths. The lengths are either full—the length of the forming bar—or sectionalized from 0.125 in. (3.175 mm) to 12.000 in. (30.48 cm). These are combined to build a specific tool length.

The leaf bar, which also attaches to the housing body and is lever operated, actually does the forming (Figure 27-1).

The leaf brake may look antiquated and simple at a glance, perhaps even appear to be an unsatisfactory piece of equipment, but it is capable of the same quality and accuracy as any other style of machine. However, it is not as fast as a standard press brake. It is a great machine for

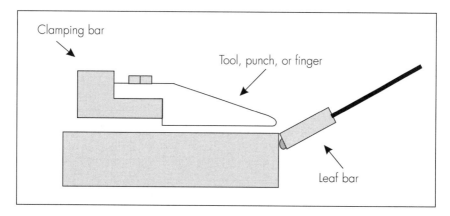

**Figure 27-1.** *Diagram of a leaf brake.*

prototype work. It is commonly found in most heating, ventilation, and air conditioning (HVAC) shops (to produce duct work).

## Three Adjustments

The leaf brake has three basic adjustments: for material thickness, backgage location, and tooling setback (not to be confused with the term, "setback," used in Chapter 7). The thickness adjustments are located on both sides of the forming bar, usually bolts with locking nuts. Without placing the material into the leaf brake, set the distance between the platen and the tooling to 0.025 in. (0.635 mm) less than the material thickness, with the forming bar locked down into place. This gives the forming bar its clamping action during forming.

The backgage is set from the front of the platen, which is the outside mold line of the bend. No allowance for the bend deduction is taken on the leaf brake since the bend allowance will be added to the flange being formed.

Figure 27-2 helps to explain the application of this bend function. As you can see, there is a distinct relationship between the center of the radius and where the workpiece needs to be clamped. Look closely at the figure and notice that all the radius and, therefore, all the bend allowance, is located on just one side of the bend. This differs from standard vee-die forming where the bend allowance and bend deduction are split almost evenly.

The bend angle and springback allowance is adjusted for at the same time through the use of a pin moved from hole to hole at 15-degree increments. An adjustment nut and bolt is used to fine tune the final bend angle. By placing the pin in the desired hole and fine tuning, an accurate and precise bend can be accomplished every time.

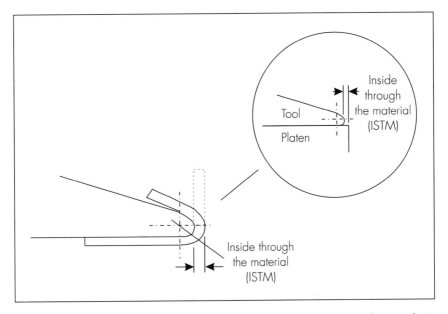

**Figure 27-2.** When setting the gap between the platen/forming bar, the punch tip needs to be set back a distance equal to that of the inside through the material (ISTM). This allows the material to form up freely without binding or pinching.

# Index